DRAW SCIENCE

COCKROACHES, STINKBUGS, AND OTHER CREEPY CRAWLERS

Reviewed and endorsed by David K. Faulkner, Entomologist from the
San Diego Natural History Museum, San Diego, California

By Christine Becker
Illustrated by Nina Kidd

Lowell House
Juvenile
Los Angeles

CONTEMPORARY BOOKS
Chicago

To Walter James and the loving memory of my mother, Bonnie Becker.

—C.B.

To my mother, who shared with me her endless fascination with the natural world.

—N.K.

Copyright © 1996 by RGA Publishing Group, Inc.
All rights reserved. No part of this work may be reproduced or transmitted in any form or by any means, electronic or mechanical, including photocopying and recording, or by any information storage or retrieval system, except as may be expressly permitted by the 1976 Copyright Act or in writing by the publisher.

Publisher: Jack Artenstein
Vice President, Juvenile Division: Elizabeth D. Amos
Director of Publishing Services: Rena Copperman
Managing Editor: Lindsey Hay
Editor in Chief, Juvenile Nonfiction: Amy Downing
Project Editor: Jessica Oifer
Art Director: Lisa-Theresa Lenthall

Lowell House books can be purchased at special discounts
when ordered in bulk for premiums and special sales.
Contact Department JH at the following address:
Lowell House Juvenile
2029 Century Park East, Suite 3290
Los Angeles, CA 90067

Manufactured in the United States of America

ISBN: 1-56565-392-0

10 9 8 7 6 5 4 3 2 1

Contents

Drawing Tips

This book shows you how to draw twenty-two different creepy crawlers. There are lots of different ways to draw, and here are just a few. You'll find some helpful hints throughout this book to help make your drawings the best they can be.

Before you begin, here are some tips that every aspiring artist should know!

- Use a large sheet of paper and make your drawing fill up the space. That way, it's easy to see what you are doing, and it will give you plenty of room to add details.

- When you are blocking in large shapes, draw by moving your whole arm, not just your fingers or your wrist.

- Experiment with different kinds of lines: do a light line, then gradually bear down for a wider, darker one. You'll find that just by changing the thickness of a line, your whole picture will look different! Also, try groups of lines, drawing all the lines in a group straight, crossing, curved, or jagged.

- Remember that every artist has his or her own style. That's why the pictures you draw won't look exactly like the ones in the book. Instead, they'll reflect your own creative touch.

- Most of all, have fun!

In drawing animals, it's always helpful to know the names of an animal's body parts. That way, you have a better understanding of your subject. For example, the illustration below shows you the names of an insect's body parts. These are helpful, not only because they teach you about insects, but they help you learn the difference between insects, bugs, and arachnids. As you learn more about the world of creepy crawlers, you'll find they share many common features. But notice that those similarities only go so far—each critter is unique in its own right.

Every bug is an insect; however, not every insect is a bug. All insects have six legs, antennae, and segmented bodies that include three parts: a head, a thorax, and an abdomen. Along with these insect characteristics, bugs also have some other more specialized ones. For example, all bugs have front wings that cover their shorter rear wings, a distinct triangular area between their wings, and a pointed mouthpart used for sucking.

Unlike insects, arachnids have eight legs, no antennae, and a two-part body made up of a cephalothorax and an abdomen. The cephalothorax of arachnids is a fused head and thorax.

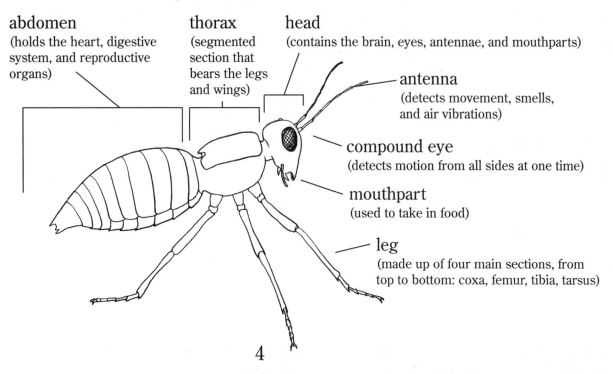

abdomen
(holds the heart, digestive system, and reproductive organs)

thorax
(segmented section that bears the legs and wings)

head
(contains the brain, eyes, antennae, and mouthparts)

antenna
(detects movement, smells, and air vibrations)

compound eye
(detects motion from all sides at one time)

mouthpart
(used to take in food)

leg
(made up of four main sections, from top to bottom: coxa, femur, tibia, tarsus)

What You'll Need

PAPER

Many kinds of paper can be used for drawing, but some are better than others. For pencil drawing, avoid newsprint or rough papers because they don't erase well. Instead, use a large pad of bond paper (or a similar type). The paper doesn't have to be thick, but it should be uncoated, smooth, and cold pressed. You can find bond paper at an art store. If you are using ink, a dull-finished, coated paper works well.

PENCILS, CHARCOAL, AND PENS

A regular school pencil is fine for the drawings in this book, but try to use one with a soft lead. Pencils with soft lead are labeled #2; #3 pencils have a hard lead. If you want a thicker lead, ask an art store clerk or your art teacher for an artist's drafting pencil.

Charcoal works well when you want a very black line, so if you're just starting to draw with charcoal, use a charcoal pencil of medium to hard grade. With it, you will be able to rub in shadows, then erase certain areas to make highlights. Work with large pieces of paper, as charcoal is difficult to control in small drawings. And remember that charcoal smudges easily!

If you want a smooth, thin ink line, try a rolling-point or a fiber-point pen. Art stores and bigger stationery stores have them in a variety of line widths and fun, bright colors.

ERASERS

An eraser is one of your most important tools! Besides removing unwanted lines and cleaning up smudges, erasers can be used to make highlights and textures. Get a soft plastic type (the white ones are good), or for very small areas, a gray kneaded eraser can be helpful. Don't take off ink with an eraser because it will ruin the drawing paper. If you must take an ink line out of your picture, use liquid whiteout.

OTHER HANDY TOOLS

Facial tissues are helpful for creating soft shadows—just go over your pencil marks with a tissue, gently rubbing the area you want smoothed out.

A square of metal window screen is another tool that can be used to make shadows. Hold it just above your paper and rub a soft pencil lead across it. Then rub the shavings from the pencil into the paper to make a smooth shadowed area in your picture. If you like, you can sharpen the edge of the shadow with your eraser.

You also will need a pencil sharpener, but if you don't have one, rub a small piece of sandpaper against the side of your pencil to keep the point sharp.

Finishing Your Drawing

As you'll see with the creepy crawlers in this book, artists must use different drawing techniques to distinguish between the various body parts and make the insects and arachnids look real. Here are some useful techniques for giving your drawings a natural look.

HATCHING

Hatching is a group of short, straight lines used to create a texture or a shadow. The hatching either can show that the surface is flat, using straight lines, or how rounded it is depending on the amount of curve in the lines. This technique is handy when texturing an insect's curved wing cases or rounded abdomen. When you draw the hatching lines close together, you create a dark shadow such as with the hairy legs of the tarantula or the abdomen of a honeybee. Look at the drawing of the cicada nymph. Notice how the lines make the abdomen appear more rounded.

STIPPLE

When you want to give your drawing a different feel, try the stipple technique—all you need is dots! This method works best with a pen, because unlike a pencil, a pen will make an even black dot by just touching the paper. The stipple technique is very similar to the way photos are printed in newspapers and books. If you look through a magnifying glass at a picture in a newspaper, you will see very tiny dots. The smaller and farther apart the dots are, the lighter the area is. The larger and closer the dots are, the darker the area. As you draw, you can make a shadow almost black by placing your stipple dots close together, as with this harvestman.

CONTROLLED SCRIBBLE

This technique allows you to put in shading, and give your drawing a fresh casual look. And, it's fun! The trick is to tilt your pencil and, using the broader side, scribble in the area. Make sure to control your scribbles so there are no large white patches among them. Use a lighter touch in the brighter shadows and gradually darken your scribbling in the deeper shade areas. Notice in this drawing of the cockroach the scribble is not used everywhere. That would be too messy looking. The tops of the wings are done in hatching, then the scribbles darken the lower part of the body and upper legs where they are in shadow. Practice this technique on your larger drawings so you can put the scribbles exactly where you want them.

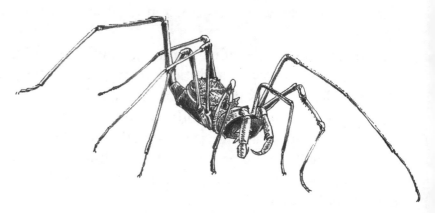

SMOOTH TONE

By using the side of your pencil, you can create a smooth texture on your creature. Starting with the areas you want to be light, stroke the paper very lightly and evenly. Put a little bit more pressure on your pencil as you move to the areas you want to be darker. If you want an area even smoother, go back and rub the pencil with a facial tissue, but rub gently! If you get smudges in areas you want to stay white, simply remove them with an eraser. Try this smooth texture on the louse.

SPECIALIZED TEXTURES

Look at the Africanized honeybee to see another way to finish a drawing. The fuzzy areas around the legs and thorax are created with lots of short strokes. Start your strokes toward the front of the body near the head and stroke toward the rear of the bee. Lift your pencil at the end of the stroke to make a thin tip. Create the shine on the abdomen by shading up to the edge of the highlight area, gradually shading less on one side of the highlight. On the other side, shade darkly. Accentuate the highlight by erasing it to remove any stray smudges or pencil marks. Highlights on the glossy wings also are created by erasing.

Now that you're armed with the basic drawing tools and techniques, you're ready to get started on the creatures in this book. What's more, you'll learn as you draw! After each drawing step, you'll find some scientific information that not only is fun and interesting to know, but also useful when it comes to drawing.

Throughout this book you'll find special Drawing Tips that will aid your progress. At the back of the book extra techniques and hints for using color, casting shadows, and placing animals in a scene show you how to make the most of your drawings.

The Cockroach has been roaming the planet for at least 345 million years, according to fossils found by scientists.

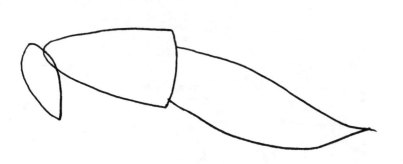

① This cockroach is rather long and slender from the side. Start by making a nose-cone shape for the thorax. Add a pointed oval for the head, bent down partly below the thorax area, and a flame shape for the abdomen.

Most humans encounter only a few different species of cockroaches, though there are over 3,500 known varieties of these crawlers in the world.

② Draw in the wedge-shaped eye curving around the top of the head, the chainlike feelers near the mouth, and the long curving shape that will be the top of the thorax and wings. Add the first sections of the legs, angling back from the head area, and a narrow triangle on the end of the abdomen.

Their flattened, oval bodies range in color from gray, brown, or black to an exotic green. Cockroaches may grow as large as 4 inches (10 centimeters) in length.

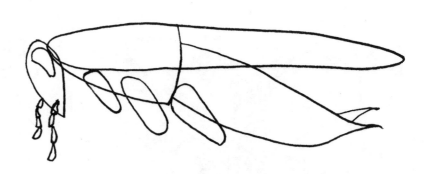

③ Add the second leg joints (don't forget the one that peeks out slightly between the abdomen and wing). Also draw the front attachment of the wings near the head.

The cockroach lays between sixteen and thirty-two eggs at a time. It deposits its eggs in a tough, yellow sac, known as an öotheca (o-eh-thee-kah). This sac is resistant to most pesticides, making these unhatched roaches quite difficult to kill.

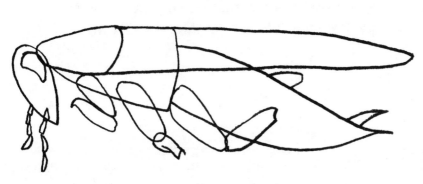

MORE SCIENCE: Cockroaches enjoy a warm climate. When outdoors, they search for damp, dark hiding places, like sewers or caves. When hiding in homes, they usually can be found in kitchens or bathrooms. At night they are attracted to the brightness of street lamps or porch lights.

In fact, so many cockroaches roamed the earth 320 to 280 million years ago that historians named the period "the Age of the Cockroaches."

④ Now add the long slender ends of the legs and jointed feet with down-curving claws. The long flexible antennae curve gracefully.

Though most cockroaches have wings, very few species fly.

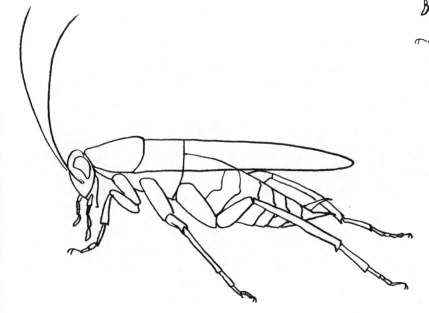

⑤ Draw in the body segments. The little bump in these lines form a ridge that runs along each side of the cockroach's body. A thin curving line below the head creates the lower part of the head.

Although they can survive up to ninety days without feeding, cockroaches will eat if food is present. Their list of favorite foods includes cardboard, paper, grease, meat, and sugary junk foods.

⑥ This cockroach is a shiny reddish-brown with matching colored wings. The pencil strokes on the wings show the tiny ridges on them, and there is a darker spot around the eye. Draw in the antennae segments and darken under the wing. Shade in the head and the upper portions of the legs, and remember to add the spiny hairs on the cockroach's legs.

Cockroaches do not sting and rarely bite. However, handling them may result in a skin irritation caused by the spines on their legs, the oils on their skin, or their feces (droppings).

The Hercules Beetle

belongs to the most abundant order of animals on earth. In fact, one in every four animal species is a beetle.

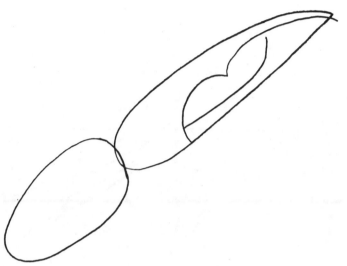

① Start with a long egg shape, the narrower end angled down. This forms the body. At the same angle, overlap a long, seed shape with a flattened bottom and a pointed top. Inside the seed shape draw a smooth scallop shape that tapers to form a slender tip on the right. Inside the scallop shape, add an up-curving line that comes close to, but does not touch the scallop. This will be the top of the "nose horn" of the beetle.

Measuring up to 7 inches (18 centimeters) in length, the hercules beetle is quite a large insect. It also can produce an unpleasant smell to ward off enemies.

② Draw three angled lines, two inside the body shape and one sticking out toward the front of the beetle. Add the flaring edges of the "helmet" between the two main body shapes, leaving a notch for the round eye. Then sketch in the eye. Finish the tapering outline of the nose horn, and add two thorn shapes on top of it.

Some hercules beetles have a uniform metallic brown color, while others are a dull greenish-gray with scattered black spots.

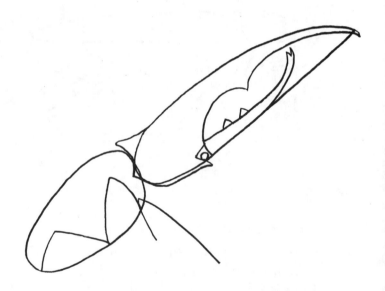

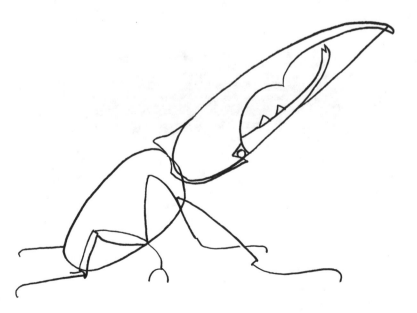

③ Add lines for the insect's feet that will end in downward-curving claws. Don't forget the small legs at the back of the body. Draw the lower edges of the hind leg within the egg-shaped body.

The name of the beetle's order (biological group), Coleoptera, means "sheath-winged." This order was given its name because of the beetle's hard, thick forewings which cover and protect its fragile body like a suit of armor.

Boasting over 350,000 different species, beetles make up forty percent of all insects on our planet.

---

④ Add lower curving edges to the legs near the front of the body, and give the feet sections and claws. Foot sections are long triangles that overlap, and leg sections have thorns that face backward. Antennae are thick, with feathery tips. Erase any unneeded lines.

A male hercules beetle locks his two horns with another male when defending territory or fighting to win a female mate.

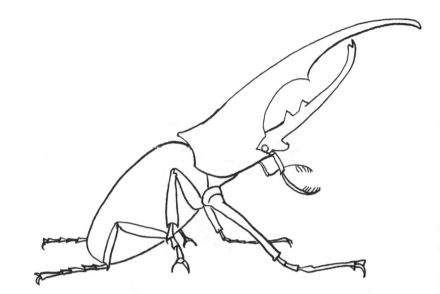

⑤ Draw in the edge of the wing case, the speckles on it, and body sections underneath. The curving lines you add on the helmet and nose horn will be the edges of the shiny highlights.

Beetles go through complete metamorphosis. This means they have four distinct stages of development. They progress from eggs to grubs (beetle larvae), to pupa, and finally to winged adults.

⑥ You can make all parts of this beetle look three-dimensional and shiny by filling in sections of the beetle as shown. Add hairs around the neck, under the head, and along the underside of the helmet. You can make the legs look rounded by shading them near the joints. Add spiky tips to each front leg. Lightly shade in speckled wing covers to give them a shiny appearance.

Unlike a bug that ingests only liquid food, this insect has mouthparts that allow it to chew and swallow solid foods.

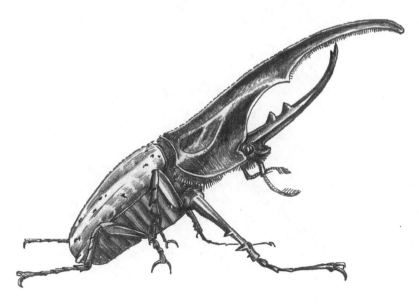

The Silverfish

may have scales, but this "fish" does not swim. The silverfish's favorite environments are laundry

① Begin this insect, viewed from above, by drawing two rounded shapes overlapping —the broader part is the body and the slimmer shape is the tail.

Silverfish are named for their silvery-gray, scaly appearance. They have compound eyes, made up of many tiny lenses, that are small and set far apart. Their bodies are soft, flat, and small, reaching only 0.4 to 0.5 inch (10 to 13 millimeters) long.

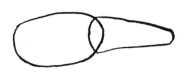

② Add the three thin, pointed parts of the tail and a flat oval for the head.

Silverfish have three bristly attachments that look like tails at the end of their abdomens. They also have limbs on their undersides that do not serve any purpose in movement.

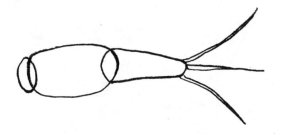

③ The antennae are longer and much straighter than the tails. The six stubs on either side of the body are the first leg joints.

Silverfish eat a variety of household items, such as books, paper, paste, as well as silk, cotton, and linen cloth. Silverfish also feed on starchy materials, such as glue, potatoes, and cereals.

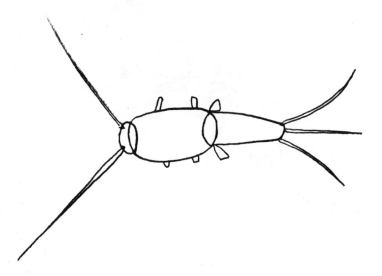

rooms and libraries, where it can eat its fill of paper and clothing material.

④ Put in the two claw-shaped tail pieces between the three thin tail parts. Add the leg's second joints, the eyes, and the edges of the body segments that curve over the back.

These insects prefer cool, damp hiding places. Some species live in the ground or in piles of leaves. Other species hide in homes and bookcases. They are rarely spotted by humans. Because they cause damage to property, silverfish are considered pests.

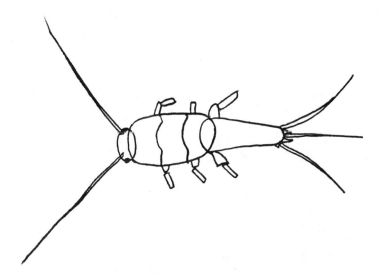

⑤ The last joints of each leg are tapering and almost pointed. Add the flattened edge around the body area, as well as the tail segments.

Old books, newspapers, and cardboard boxes carried into homes can contain silverfish. This quick creature also may crawl indoors through a crack or hole in the wall.

⑥ This insect gets its name because it can look shiny silver. You can make yours look metallic by leaving a clean white strip along the back. Use dark shading along the edge of the insect, and lighten shading as you near the center of the back. Put in a fine fringe of hairs all around the head and body, twiggy shapes on the tail, and hairs on the legs.

Silverfish are one of the most ancient insect groups on earth. Because scientists believe they were living before the dinosaurs, they are sometimes called "living fossils."

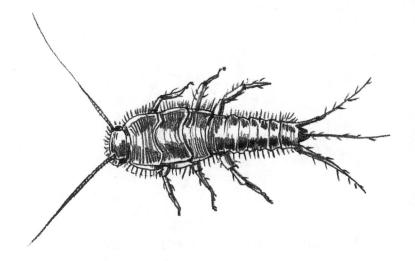

Imported Fire Ants

arrived in the United States between the late 1930s and early 1940s from their native country of Brazil. Since their

① Start the abdomen by creating an ice cream cone. The rounded shape on top of the cone becomes the general shape of the body.

Fire ants use their sharp, three-pronged mandibles to pierce the skin of potential prey or those that the ants perceive as a threat. Next, they use the stinger on the end of their abdomen to inject poisonous venom into the bite site.

② Draw a line through the center of the egg and cone, then curve it out to the right. Draw the squarish shape, which is the head, centering the line on the face. Add the oval thorax shape connecting head and tail.

Although ants have eyes, their vision is poor. Instead, they rely almost exclusively on their antennae to smell and navigate.

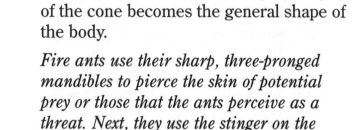

③ Draw the beads within the cone. Then add the relatively heavy first leg joints. Now add the eyes.

Male fire ants possess wings throughout life. Fertile females use their wings just once, to meet a male for airborne mating. Once fertilized, she drops to the ground and uses her legs to break off her four wings. This impregnated ant then becomes a queen and spends the rest of her life in the soil, laying eggs and being taken care of by worker ants.

MORE SCIENCE: Each species of ant secretes a chemical, called a pheromone, that is unique to its own group. Smelled and tasted by other members, pheromones pass messages that are used for identification, mating, and defense.

arrival, these ants have caused great distress among farmers. Fire ants build large, hard homes, called mounds, that damage field equipment, and their stings have proved painful and sometimes deadly to livestock and people.

---

④ Add the second leg joints (don't forget the one showing behind the rear of the body and the one that shows just below the ant's left eye). Next draw in the flat curving pincers under the head.

While beehives usually have only one queen per hive, a large colony of ants living in a mound may have thousands of queens.

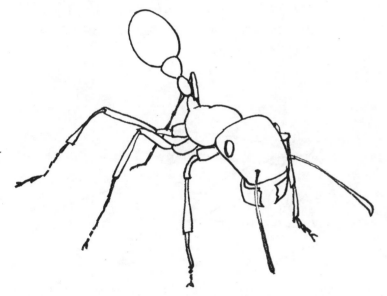

⑤ Draw in the very important antennae, the thin lower leg sections, and jointed feet. You should be able to see five out of the six feet. Erase any extra lines.

Ants have two-chambered stomachs. The first section, the crop, acts as a food-storing "social stomach." Part of the food remains in the crop and the rest passes into the second chamber, the midgut, to be digested by the ant.

⑥ These ants are shiny on their legs and body with a slightly grooved head. Each eye, body section, and leg segment should have a white highlight—roundish for the rounded shapes and long and skinny for the slim leg shapes. Add the sparse hairs on the forelegs and sections of the antennae.

To share food from a "social stomach," a hungry ant approaches a donor, an ant that has a full crop. The hungry ant strokes the donor's liplike structure, which is called the labium, and the donor ant then vomits its liquid food into the waiting mouthpart of the receiving ant.

The Mosquito
endangers human lives more than any other insect.
Every year, besides inflicting swollen, itchy bites,

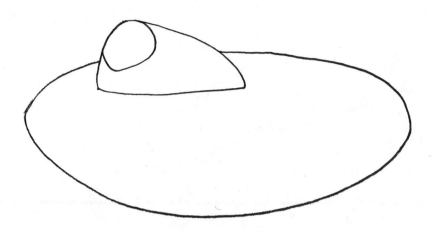

① Start by drawing a large, flattened oval shape. Add a smaller, rounded shape near the top of the oval, and an egg shape inside of that (which forms the thorax).

It is only the fertile female mosquito that survives on the blood of birds and mammals. She needs the protein contained in blood to nourish her developing eggs. Male mosquitoes, and female mosquitoes that are not bearing eggs, feed on plant juices, nectar, and water.

② From the top part of the egg, follow the curve down to the right to create a banana-shaped body. Add a circle for the head on the left, and sketch in a very long, straight oval for the wing. Three sticklike shapes at the top make the first joints of the far legs. The near leg sections are two thick Vs, with an extra stroke in the center.

The female uses her sharp stylet, or long needlelike beak, to pierce the skin, inject her saliva (which prevents scabs from forming over the wound), and then suck out her victim's blood. The entire feeding process takes only a couple of minutes.

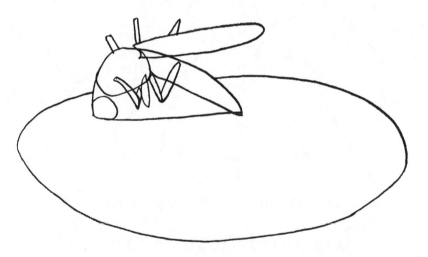

③ Add the long, slim antennae and the bent sucking-needle mouth which curves down. Now put in the second joint of both the far legs and the near legs. The far rear leg can be seen above and below the wing. Notice how all the legs come from one place under the thorax.

When a mosquito sucks the blood of a victim infected with a disease, it obtains the blood-borne parasites that cause the disease. These parasites multiply within the mosquito's own digestive system and spread to other body parts. As she injects her infectious saliva into her next victims, she passes on the parasites to each one of them.

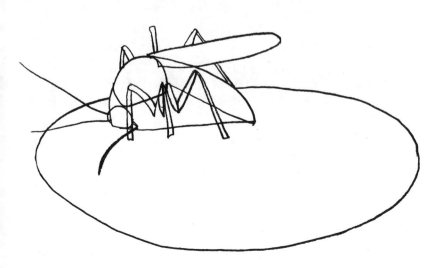

mosquitoes infect millions of people worldwide with diseases such as yellow fever and malaria.

④ Add a large oval within the round, head shape to become the eye. Then draw the remaining sections of the long slender legs. Use the large oval as a guide for the ends of the feet.

Female mosquitoes lay their eggs in water. While some eggs float individually, others join together to make "rafts" that drift along as a group until they hatch.

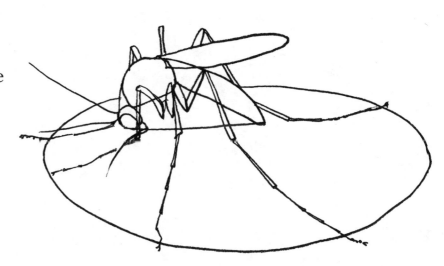

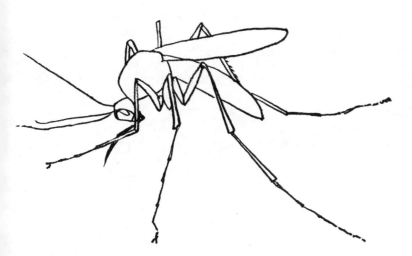

⑤ Add the hair on the far back leg, as well as the small shape inside the eye. Erase extra lines.

Mosquito larvae are called wrigglers because their bodies squirm around while feeding. When wrigglers hatch from their eggs, they live just below the surface of the water. Because larvae need oxygen, they must use breathing tubes located on their abdomens to reach air above the water's surface.

⑥ This mosquito has a hairy thorax and a dark upper body. Lightly shade the wing, leaving white highlights on it. Where the leg sections join together, make your shading darker. The antennae and the rear legs are uneven and twiggy.

In nature, the mosquito is prey to many different animals, including birds, bats, lizards, and fish. One species of dragonfly has earned the name "mosquito hawk," because it can capture and devour as many as one hundred mosquitoes in a short period of time!

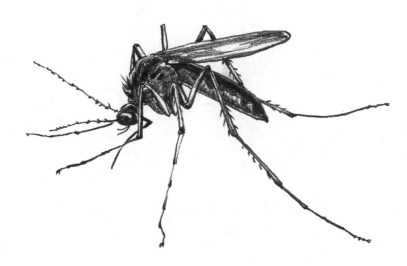

The Blow Fly is just one of the 80,000 known species of flies that exist throughout the world. Because it lives in filthy

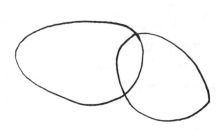

① This fly has a bullet-shaped abdomen (left), and a flattened oval (right) for the thorax. Overlap the two shapes as shown.

A blow fly searches for fresh meat on which to lay its eggs. It may also lay eggs in the open wounds of animals. When the eggs hatch into fly larvae, called maggots, this can cause infection and infestation (the invasion of maggots).

② For the head, add a fat triangle that overlaps the thorax. Also draw in a curved petal shape that touches the back of the head for the guidelines of the wings.

All blow flies undergo the four distinct stages of a complete metamorphosis: They exist first as eggs, then as maggots in what is called the larval stage. The flies then go through a pupal stage, where they continue to grow within a cocoonlike structure, before they emerge in their adult form.

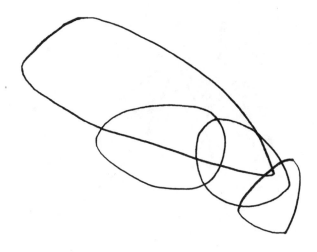

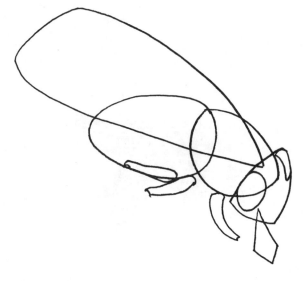

③ Outline the bulging eyes at the outer edges of the head, and hang a diamond shape under the head for its mouth. Sketch the upper sections of the three visible legs, with the front leg curving toward the center of the body.

The maggots of blow flies are scavengers. They live in garbage, feces, and the dead bodies of animals.

DRAWING TIP: If you darken in some of the spaces between the veins, leaving some light streaks, it will show that the wings are shiny and see-through.

habitats, the blow fly is prone to spreading diseases and infections that affect both animals and humans.

---

④ After you add the second leg sections, outline the wings in the guidelines. Notice how these lines start at the edges of the petal shape, and then curve and cross back to where the wings fasten at the thorax. Add the edges of the body plates just behind the head, as well as the wedge-shaped forehead.

Although blow fly maggots usually feed on dead flesh, they sometimes invade and eat healthy tissue, causing extreme pain in the affected animal.

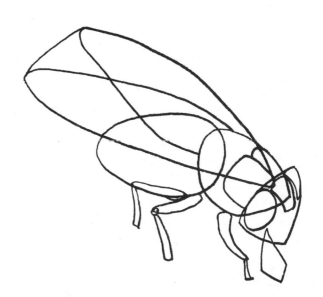

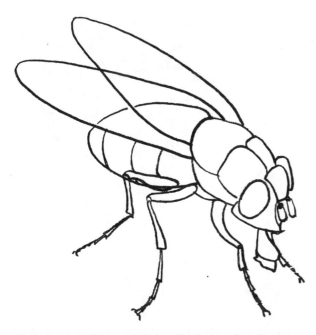

⑤ Finish the smallest joints of the legs that curve outward, ending with the clawed feet. Draw in the slightly curved body segments visible below the wings. Add the lower part of the mouth, as well as two clublike antennae right in front of the eyes. Erase unneeded lines.

The body of the blow fly is a metallic blue or green, and it is covered with thick, black hairs known as setae (see-tee).

⑥ To finish the fly you can darken the body using short, thick hatching strokes to emphasize the body segments and plates on the back. The fly's wings are somewhat transparent, so sketch in very light lines to give them a scaly texture. Draw thick, crisscrossing lines to make the dark areas on the eyes. Then erase a small area in the center of the eye for the shiny highlight. Finally, add spiky hairs around the body, head, and legs.

Some scientists believe that flies cannot actually identify images. Instead, their eyes detect movements and changes in lighting. Other experts state that flies perceive slightly distorted images with their compound eyes.

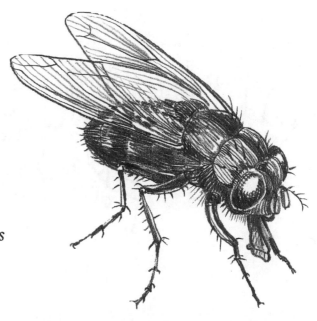

The Flea is a tiny yet powerful bloodsucker that has troubled humans and their pets all over the world for many years. Just mentioning its

① Start the body with a broad leaf shape that overlaps a small bullet shape for the head.

Fleas measure only 0.1 inch (2.5 millimeters) in length and have long, powerful hind legs that give them incredible leaping ability. They can jump up to 14 inches (36 centimeters) from side to side and almost 12 inches (30 centimeters) straight up. This is equivalent to a human jumping up 550 feet (168 meters) in the air.

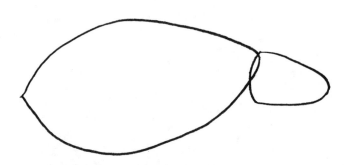

② Draw the first section of the legs closest to you. Add small connector joints and then the bean-shaped second section of the legs. At the bottom, further connect the head and body together with a thin line.

Fleas reproduce quickly, laying up to six hundred eggs in one month on their host, furniture, or in carpet. Six to twelve days after the eggs are deposited, flea larvae hatch.

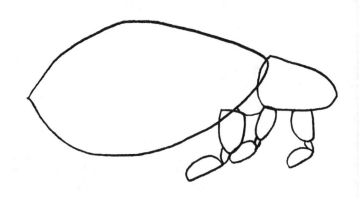

③ Put in the round eye and feathery mouthparts, as well as the lines that curve over the back, halfway down the body. These show the edges of the outer covering's sections. Long triangles form the next leg sections. Add the portions of the other three legs that show from the far side of the body.

Strong hooks on its head and thorax help anchor the flea to its host. Humans, cats, dogs, rodents, and other mammals serve as hosts for many species of fleas. Some flea species feed mostly on birds.

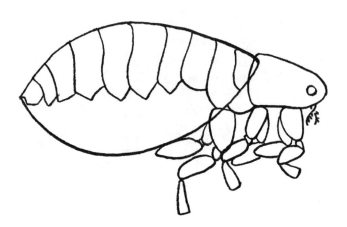

④ Finish sketching in the lower abdomen sections, the end of the head, and the jointed legs with hooked feet.

Russians have trained fleas to perform tricks. By using a magnifying glass and a silk thread as a leash, trainers can teach fleas to juggle, leap through hoops, and drag heavy objects.

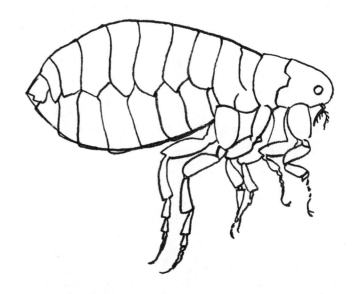

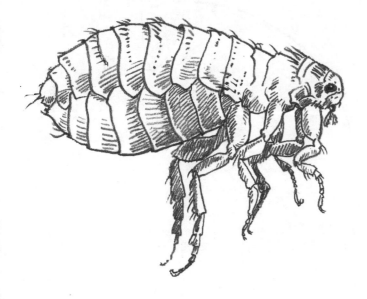

⑤ Use short dark hatching lines to shade the far legs, the underside of the body plates, and around the head. Add the spiky hairs along each section, at the rear of the head, and on the legs.

Extremely strong insects, fleas can lift and drag objects that weigh more than 150 times their body weight.

MORE SCIENCE: Fleas carry both typhus and tapeworms. In fact, infected rat fleas have been blamed for spreading the bubonic plague to humans. This plague, known as The Black Death, killed between fifty and seventy-five percent of the populations of Europe and Western Asia in the fourteenth century.

The Head Louse

breeds year-round on a person's warm head. Human lice, which include both head lice and

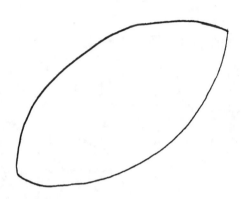

① Draw a long football shape for the abdomen of this insect, which is seen from above.

Each louse is a grayish-white wingless insect. It is round and flat and grows only 0.04 to 0.16 inch (1 to 4 millimeters) in length.

② Add a bulging square shape that will be the thorax area.

With claws at the end of their short, stout legs, head lice can only survive when they are firmly attached to their hosts' hair and feeding from the scalp. Body lice, however, can survive away from the body, such as on clothing and linens.

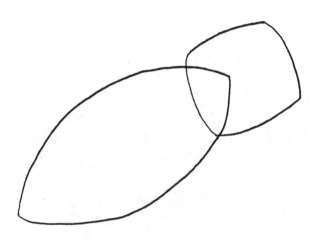

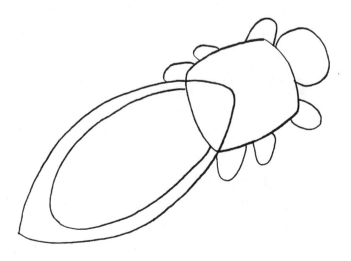

③ The six stout legs stick out from under the thorax. Add a partial circle for the head area and an oval within the outline of the abdomen. This will be used as a guide for the body lobes.

Lice lay small, white eggs, called nits, which become attached to strands of hair. They hatch in about one week.

body lice, are parasites that live off the blood of their human hosts.

④ Draw a blunt point on the front of the head, as well as the heavy-looking antennae curving inward. Add the second leg segments, with the two rear pairs of legs curving in as if they are going under the body.

Lice are passed from person to person by direct contact. Head lice are passed very easily on shared combs, brushes, or hats. Borrowing clothing, towels, or sheets from an infected person will spread body lice.

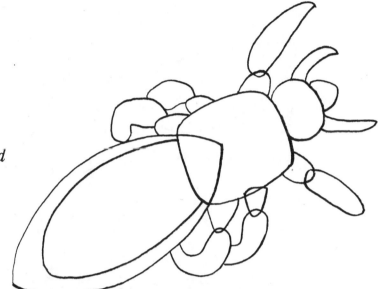

⑤ Add the body lobes as bulges between the football-shaped abdomen and the inner outline. Draw them larger toward the rear of the body. Add the eyes as bumps on either side of the head. Also draw the antennae segments and shape each of the segments on the legs. Be sure to include the claws of the forelegs. Erase all unnecessary lines.

Signs of head lice include: a constantly itching scalp, white nits attached to strands of hair, and/or brown spots of lice droppings seen on the shoulders when light-colored clothes are worn.

⑥ This is a lumpy, light-colored insect with smooth edges. Use the side of the pencil to create a smooth tone. Then rub the shading with a tissue to smear it to a very light gray. Legs and head are darker near the center of the body. Add sparse bristles.

Signs of body lice include: continual itchiness of the skin, reddened bite sites that are painful and itchy, brown spots of feces near the armpits, and/or scabbing caused by lice bites.

The Praying Mantis, sometimes called the mantid, may appear to be praying toward heaven,

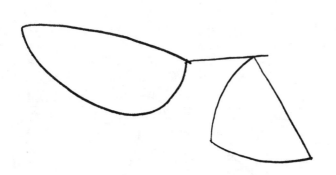

① Start with the body shape, a half-egg shape placed horizontally. From this, draw a line, angled up slightly, and hang a triangle from the line.

One of the few insects capable of turning its head almost completely around, the mantis uses this, as well as the spines on its front legs, as advantages while hunting.

② Link the two large shapes with a long, oval shape (the mantis's neck). On the right side of the body, construct a smaller triangle for the insect's head.

Mantises will use their strong, biting mouthparts to consume such prey as moths, caterpillars, and various other bugs. Larger mantises even eat lizards, frogs, and small birds.

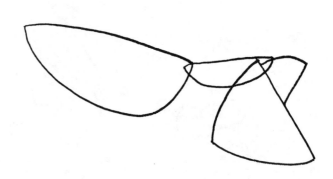

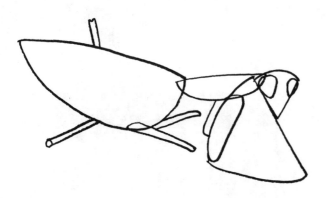

③ Draw the four slender first joints of the mantis's legs, sticking out from under the body. Draw in the eyes at the corners of the triangular head. Add a long oval inside of the body for the insect-trapping forelegs. Don't forget the farther leg that shows just slightly, below the mantis's neck.

While mating, the female often throws the male off her back and bites off his head. The headless male body once again mounts the female and finishes the mating process. Afterward, the female devours the rest of the male's body.

MORE SCIENCE: Because they prey on so many insects that destroy crops and plants, farmers welcome the presence of praying mantises.

but it actually holds its front legs in this upraised position so it can strike its unsuspecting victims with lightning speed.

---

④ Add the second broad section of the front legs, and the second slim section of the hind legs. Draw the edge of the mantis's leaflike wing that sweeps along its back, as well as the straighter line that is a rib on the wing that folds under the top wing.

In the autumn female mantises attach their eggs to weeds and twigs. The protective egg cases, which are described as papier-mâché-like in appearance, house the eggs through winter.

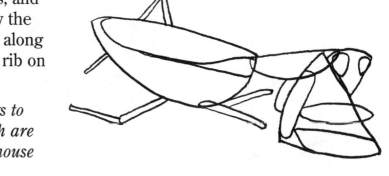

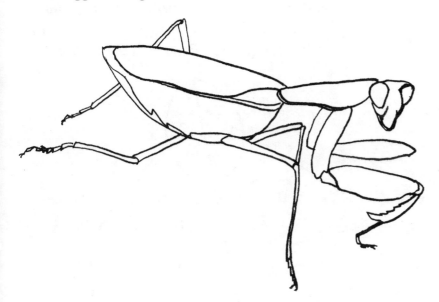

⑤ Finish the legs and feet of the insect using smaller and smaller joints and claws on the ends of the feet. The forelegs have a row of spines used to trap insects. Smooth and finish the head and the "elbow" joints on the forelegs. Shape the neck, making it broader over the leg attachments. Next add the "teeth" along the lower edge of the body. Erase all unneeded lines.

When they hatch, the young nymphs are very hungry. If food is not readily available, mantis nymphs will eat each other.

⑥ Darken the eyes of the mantis, and add the hairlike antennae. Draw in ridges around the edges of the wings and the neck plate, as well as along the rear edge of the forelegs. Add two short tail pieces. Shade in the body to look like leaves with smooth veining. Shadow under the edges of every body part to help make the mantis look three-dimensional. Now your mantis looks ready for hunting!

To prevent being preyed upon, this insect can change its colors to match its surroundings, making it harder to detect. If spotted, the mantis uses its wings to escape from predators.

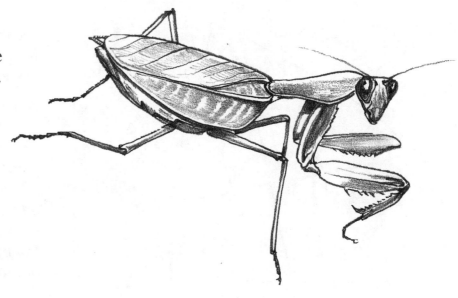

The Killer Bee (Africanized Honeybee)

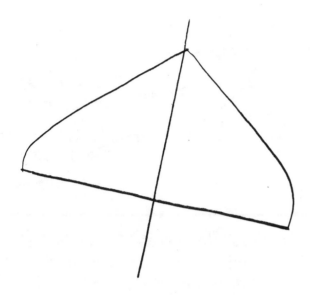

① Use a ruler or other straightedge to make a slanting line. Then draw a glider shape as the outline of the bee's wings.

Killer bees become aggravated very easily. After a single irritated Africanized bee stings a victim, it releases an alarm scent, called a pheromone, that signals hundreds to thousands of bees to attack. The venom from the sting of the killer bee is no more potent than other honeybees. It is the huge number of bees attacking at one time that poses the greatest danger to the victim.

② Add an oval at the top pointed end. Then, leaving some space in between, draw a bullet shape for the bee's abdomen.

The fierce tempers of killer bees drive them to stay angry and attack much longer than European honeybees. Killer bees will also chase their enemies for up to 1 mile, a much greater distance than other species of honeybees.

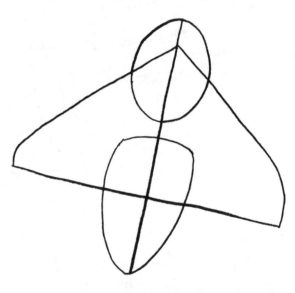

③ A curving, cap shape at the top will form the head. Leaving some space around the body, draw the wedge-shaped sections of the legs.

Killer bees live in highly structured colonies that are organized into castes, or social groupings. The queen bees (fertile females) and the drones (fertile males) make up the reproductive caste. The drones fertilize the queen and then die soon after mating. Sterile females form the worker bee caste and perform every other task in the colony, from making the honeycombs to feeding the queen to producing the honey.

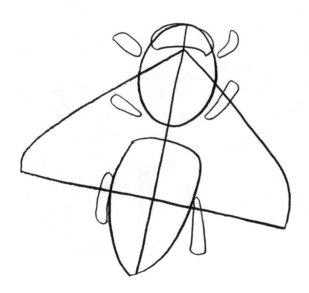

MORE SCIENCE: Killer bees' aggressive behavior and decreased honey production make them poor candidates for beekeepers.

is the offspring of two different species of bees, African queen bees, and European honeybees. The Africanized honeybee contains traits of both species, but its most well-known characteristic is its highly aggressive behavior.

④ Within the glider shape, complete the club-shaped forewings. Add the big eyes at the outer edges of the head, and the short thick antennae. Draw the next sections of the hind legs.

Because they live in warm climates, Africanized honeybees store less honey for food to survive a cold winter. Spending less time making honey than other species, the queen and some members of her colony tend to find new nest sites more frequently.

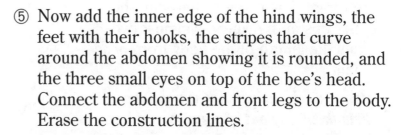

⑤ Now add the inner edge of the hind wings, the feet with their hooks, the stripes that curve around the abdomen showing it is rounded, and the three small eyes on top of the bee's head. Connect the abdomen and front legs to the body. Erase the construction lines.

When all the Africanized honeybees in a colony suddenly abandon their nest together it is called absconding. Killer bees abscond when there is a low food supply in the area around their colony.

⑥ Complete the bee by darkening its broad stripes and its legs. Draw in the antennae segments and darken the antennae and eyes. Honeybees are very furry on the thorax, head, and legs. Use short light strokes to draw the fur. Thicken the top edge of the forewing with a second line. Then add the veins which make the wings appear stiff.

Every species of honeybees communicates among themselves. They use special movement patterns, circles, and "dances" to alert fellow colony members to the location of flowers and the quality and quantity of nectar.

The Silkworm Moth is closely related to the butterfly. However, there are several distinct differences between the two. Moth caterpillars spin a

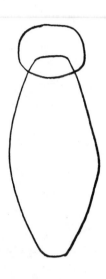

① This is a view of the silkworm moth from directly above. Sketch in the long, thick body and short thorax, overlapping them slightly.

The impregnated female silkworm moth lays her eggs on mulberry leaves that provide nourishment for the larvae once they hatch.

② Add a smaller flat oval for the moth's head, and two sweeping triangles for the wings. The distance between the upper tips of the wings is almost two times the length of the body from head to tail.

After a week caterpillars (moth larvae) chew their way out of the eggs and begin their greedy feast. In their first day of life, caterpillars can stuff themselves with up to twice their weight in leaves. As a result, they gain a lot of weight very quickly.

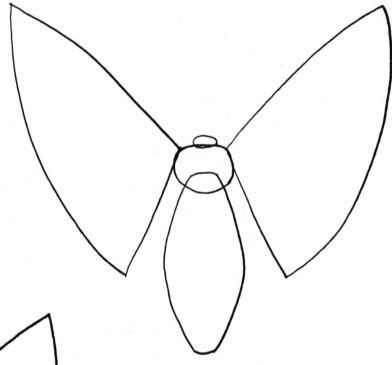

③ Add the tiny eyes at either end of the head oval, and outline the lower part of the triangles with petal-shaped hind wings. These attach to the lower part of the thorax on either side.

A silkworm larva will shed its outer covering six times before spinning its cocoon. With each shed, or molt, the caterpillar grows larger.

silken cocoon to occupy during their pupal stage. Butterfly pupa live in a different kind of enclosed shelter, called a chrysalis. Moths have threadlike or feathery antennae, while butterflies possess antennae that have round knobs on the end.

④ Draw the larger forewings, overlapping the hind wings and filling up the large triangles. Add the curving antennae, not quite touching the forewings.

When the caterpillar is ready to begin its next stage as a pupa, it will use its mouth glands to create silk thread and spin a cocoon around itself. The silkworm caterpillar may produce a single strand of silk up to 1 mile long.

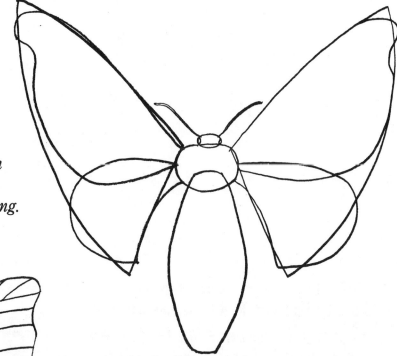

⑤ Draw in the body segments, curving around the thick shape. Copy the wing veins, each a mirror image of the facing wing. The pattern of veins tells scientists exactly what kind of silkworm moth this is.

During the two to three weeks spent inside the cocoon, the caterpillar undergoes many changes to prepare for its final stage of life. One such change is the development of wings.

⑥ Finally, put in the short fringe of fur around each wing and the long, smooth fur on the body. This moth is nearly all white, so keep shading light. Lightly erase shading down the center of the moth's body to emphasize the moth's whiteness. Small patches of lines within the wing cells show that the wings are actually opaque, or not see-through.

The silk from the silkworm's cocoon is used to create the very beautiful, soft silk fabric that is woven into clothing and linens.

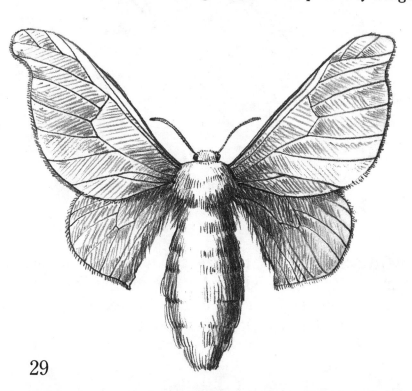

29

The Thirteen-Year Cicada Nymph (Locust)

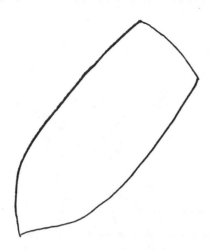

① The abdomen of the cicada nymph is pointed at the tail. Draw it like a pointed bullet.

There are over 1,500 species of cicadas in the world. While this particular periodical species lives for thirteen years, the life cycle of another periodical species is seventeen years. Other species of cicada live only two to five years.

② Add a blunt wedge for the thorax and head, and a triangle for the forewing.

The nickname "locust" is used to describe both the thirteen- and seventeen-year cicadas. Yet, the only true locusts are the migratory grasshoppers. True locusts devour plants and crops, causing great damage, so they are considered among the worst insect pests.

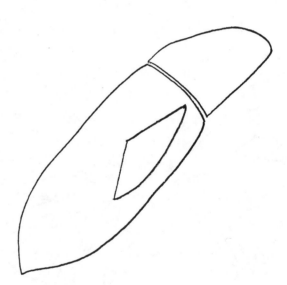

③ Put in the eyes, as well as the triangular section on the top of the bullet shape. Also add the partially hidden hind wing and the first thick leg joints.

The cicada causes damage to trees by slitting twigs and depositing its eggs inside the limbs. Because thousands of cicadas may continually invade a single tree or a group of trees, the damage they create is severe and long-lasting.

MORE SCIENCE: The male cicada uses membranes on the side of its abdomen to produce a "song" that sounds like a loud buzzing or humming. This song is used both as a mating call, to attract female cicadas, and as a form of protection. When a large group of cicadas "sing their songs," the sound drives away birds, their primary predator.

develops slowly, taking a full thirteen years to reach adulthood. Upon maturing, a winged cicada emerges from its nymphal case between May and June. Over the next six weeks it feeds on plants, mates, lays eggs, and then dies.

④ The antennae curve in and then out on either side of the head. Outline the rear of the thorax section and add the second joint of the nearest legs. Also draw the second joint of the far, front legs.

During damp weather the eggs of the cicada hatch into nymphs, and their twig dwellings break off and fall to the ground. The brown, bulky nymphs live in the soil and feed off the sap of tree roots.

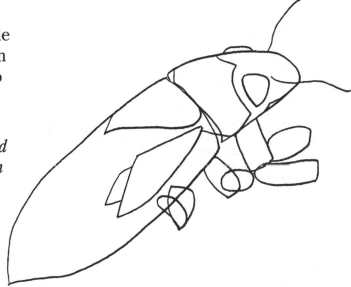

⑤ Finish the legs with jagged feet ending in long stout hooks. These are for holding onto trees. Notice how each leg section comes out from inside the one before it. Draw lines wrapping around the abdomen to show the sections. Erase any extra lines.

As they near maturity, nymphs work their way up a tree and fasten themselves tightly to the trunk. There they begin the molting, or shedding, process.

⑥ Darken in the eye with a black center and a white highlight. The eye will stand out more with a very dark rim. Use groups of short curving lines to shade the plates and ridges of the hard body covering. Where there is a shadow, make your edging line very thick and dark. Leave a white stripe along the upper side for a highlight.

The cicada's head, thorax, and abdomen tend to be black with green markings. Some species have red eyes and red vein markings on their transparent wings.

31

The Mottled Sand Grasshopper

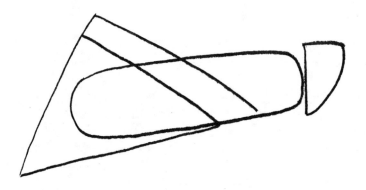

① The body of this insect begins with a long oval. Position a rounded triangular shape for the head and draw two larger triangles that overlap part of the body.

When touched, this grasshopper spits a brownish fluid that people commonly call "tobacco juice" to defend itself. This juice is actually the contents of its stomach and its texture is similar to a human's vomit.

② Add the second, long oval with a piece cut out of it for the wing cases. Draw in the turkey drumstick-shaped jumping legs inside the triangles, as well as the first joints of the three other visible legs. Add the large oval eye and on top of the head, a small bump which holds the second eye.

The mottled sand grasshopper is part of the family of short-horned grasshoppers, which are grasshoppers that have short antennae. The mottled sand grasshopper has an auditory, or hearing, organ on its first abdominal segment. This means that it hears through the trunk of its body.

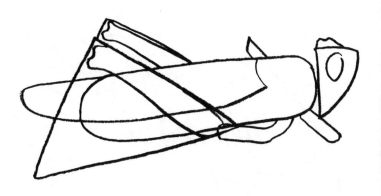

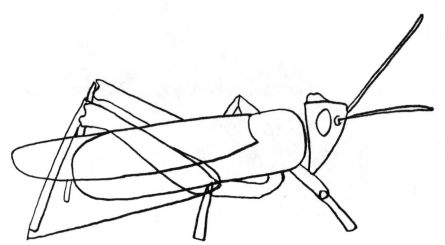

③ Draw the thin rear leg segments of the jumping legs, the second sections of the other legs, and the antennae.

Most grasshoppers eat plants, though some will eat insects. Both wingless nymphs and adult grasshoppers can eat sixteen times their weight in food in one day.

is just one species in the large grasshopper family. Its gray, brown, or beige coloring helps to camouflage, or hide, this grasshopper from possible predators.

---

④ Finish the jumping legs by adding the jointed feet. The other legs have tiny horse-hoof shaped feet. Draw a line from the top of the head to the body. Add the mouthpart and the lower edge of the top wing. Put in the curving edges of the abdomen sections.

Most nymphs molt, shed their outer covering, six times in about sixty days until they reach their full adult size. Wings develop gradually with functional wings appearing after the last molt.

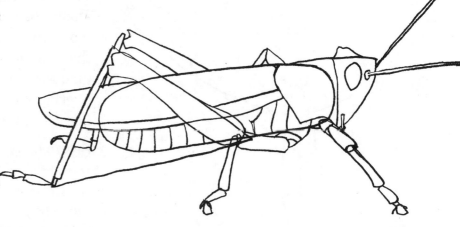

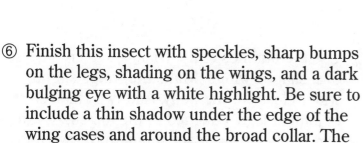

⑤ Refine the shape of the broad collar, with movable sections. Then erase all extra lines.

Grasshoppers have two sets of wings. The front set covers the entire body, and is longer, narrower, and thicker than the back wings. The grasshopper uses its more delicate hind wings to fly. When resting, the grasshopper folds its hind wings under its front wings.

⑥ Finish this insect with speckles, sharp bumps on the legs, shading on the wings, and a dark bulging eye with a white highlight. Be sure to include a thin shadow under the edge of the wing cases and around the broad collar. The antennae should be segmented.

Grasshoppers can survive in almost every type of climate from mountaintop to rain forests.

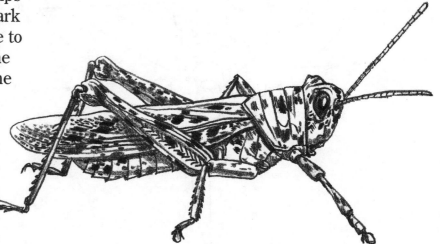

MORE SCIENCE: Grasshoppers make a noise or "song" when they rub their legs and wings together. This act is called stridulation. These songs have three main purposes: calling for mates, warning other insects that predators may be near, and for males to scare competing males.

The Dragonfly **is the most ancient flying insect known. The earliest fossils of these graceful aerialists are almost**

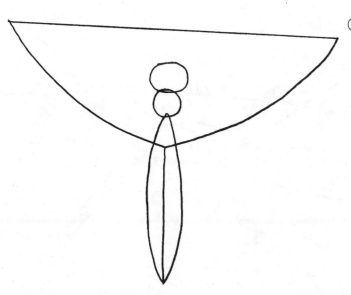

① This is a view from directly above. Draw a long petal shape for the abdomen and a circle for the thorax. To make the head, add a slightly flattened circle larger than and on top of the round thorax. Sketch an upside-down triangle with slightly curving sides, overlapping the abdomen section. Draw a middle line from the tip of the triangle down to the tail.

A dragonfly may grow up to 5 inches (13 centimeters) in length. North American dragonflies have wings that stretch as far as 4 inches (10 centimeters) across, but other tropical species have wingspans of up to 8 inches (20 centimeters).

② Overlap a second triangle below the first. Make its lower tip about halfway between the top and bottom of the abdomen. This should be a bit shorter (from tip to base) than the first triangle but also a bit wider from left tip to right. Draw a rounded loop around the upper end of the abdomen shape where the two triangles overlap.

Dragonflies have two large compound eyes, which have as many as 50,000 lenses each. They quickly detect movement and can spot prey up to 40 feet (12 centimeters) away.

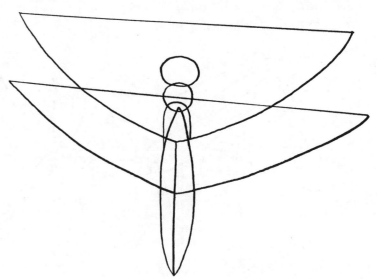

③ Use the outlines of the triangles to create long, oval-shaped wings. Make the wings slightly wider closer to the body. Add two small pairs of jointed legs, attached to the top set of wings and the head. Each set should have two hooks on the ends for feet. The curving lines on the head form the edge of the eyes, which cover the front part of the head. Put in the short thin antennae.

Dragonflies' bodies are brilliantly colored; they may be green, yellow, blue, red, or black. Their wings are transparent, so their many veins are clearly visible.

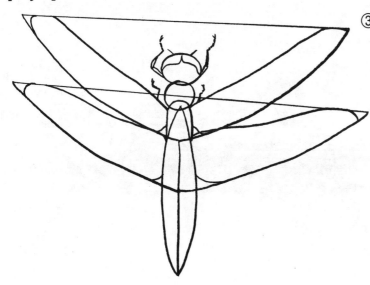

MORE SCIENCE: Its close relative, the damselfly, can be separated from the dragonfly by its slower flight, its smaller size, and its habit of holding its wings vertically while at rest.

④ Copy the partial circle on the lower part of the head and the patterns along the back of the abdomen. Create the first vein by adding an inner edge on the top part of each wing. Between the front edge and the first vein on each wing are two solid black marks. The rest of the wings are clear.

An expert flier, the dragonfly can stop instantly in midair and even fly backward. Some species have been clocked flying at speeds of up to 35 miles (90 kilometers) per hour.

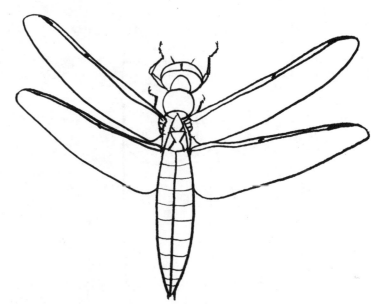

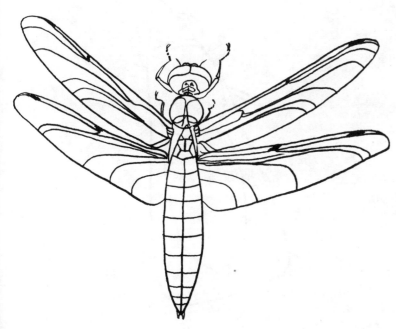

⑤ Add the mouthpart between the antennae, as well as the head markings. Also draw the pattern on the thorax and additional lines on the back. Then put in the elegant pattern of curved wing veins.

The female lays as many as eight hundred eggs at a time by dipping her abdomen into the water and squirting the eggs onto underwater rocks or leafy plants. During this two-minute process, the male, in order to protect the female and his offspring, either floats above the female or remains attached to her until the egg laying process is complete.

⑥ Finish this insect by darkening the eyes, thorax, and abdomen, leaving white space as shown. Draw in the fringe of fine hairs around the body and upper legs. Also shade in small squarish shapes that show the spaces between the thinnest veins within the clear veins.

By day, dragonflies are found near ponds and streams, hovering around rocks or sticks. At night, they usually perch themselves in weeds, tall plants, and grass.

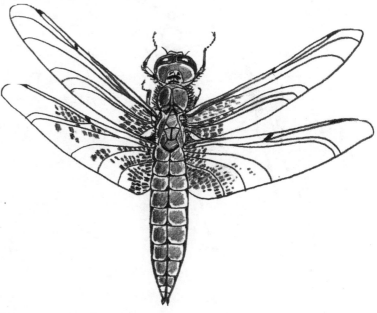

Paper Wasps

are social insects. This means they live in colonies where a queen rules, the members share food, and the young are raised by the entire group. The paper wasp

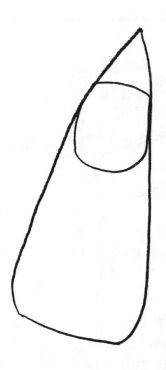

① Begin with a long triangle with rounded lower tips. Place a shortened oval inside this triangle, toward the sharp point.

Every paper wasp community must be rebuilt each year, because all the wasps, except fertilized females, die during the winter. The surviving females then become the queens and start their own new colonies.

② Add a pointed bullet shape for the abdomen, a slightly curved oval for the head, and two of the three pairs of legs, visible in this overhead view.

The common name of these wasps, paper wasps, comes from the paperlike appearance of their single-layered nests. Their nests can be found hanging from the eaves of buildings or patio ceilings.

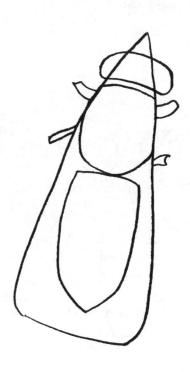

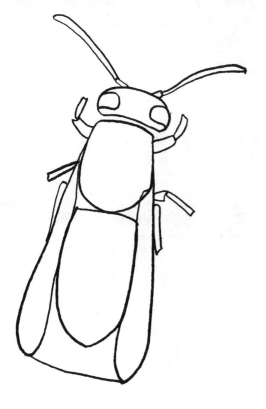

③ Now that you've drawn the outer edge of the wings with the triangle, make the inner edge, slightly pointing the wings in the rear (bottom of your drawing). Add the next joint of the legs, as well as the eyes, which wrap around the insect's head. Draw the broad antennae.

While building the nest, the queen combines peeled fibers of dry wood or paper with her saliva. The queen then will drink water so that she can later vomit it on the nest. When this shiny vomit coating dries, it helps make the nest water-resistant.

36

community is different from other social colonies, though, because it must be rebuilt each spring.

---

④ Add the joints and budlike shapes of the feet. Put in shapes on the thorax (where this insect is bright yellow). Add the three small simple eyes on top of the head.

Only the female wasp has a stinger. She uses this stinger to defend her colony. Differing from killer bees, wasps do not sting once and then die. Instead, one wasp may inflict multiple stings on a victim.

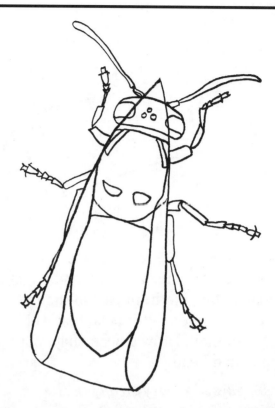

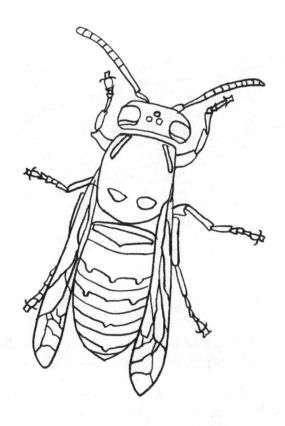

⑤ Add the sections of the antennae and the veins in the wings. Create the outlines of the stripes where this insect is colored black and yellow. Erase unneeded lines.

Paper wasps' 1-inch-long bodies range from brown to black and have orange or yellow stripes. Males have a whitish or yellow face while females' faces are brown. Their wings tend to be a transparent reddish-brown color.

⑥ Fill in the furry, dark thorax and head. Add fringes on the legs. Shade in the areas on the wasp's head and thorax as shown.

Normally, a paper wasp flies slowly and aimlessly. Yet, when it is about to attack, the wasp will fly very fast, speeding directly toward its aggressor. A similar darting flight pattern may be seen in the late summer, during mating season.

The Assassin Bug

is a hunter of other insects and was given its name because of its ability to kill its victims so skillfully.

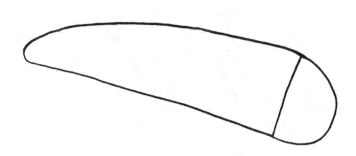

① Start with a petal shape that curves downward slightly. Draw a line across the broad end.

Assassin bugs range in color from orange to a brownish-black. Some species have black and white stripes present on their heads and legs.

② Using the petal shape as a base, add a fat oval that will be the front part of the body, and a longer, fatter petal that will be the abdomen. Draw a bean shape for the upturned head.

Assassin bugs also vary greatly in size and shape. They measure from 0.2 inch (5 millimeters) to the size of a silver dollar. They commonly have fairly long bodies and heads, though some species may be oval in shape.

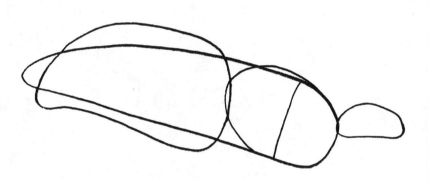

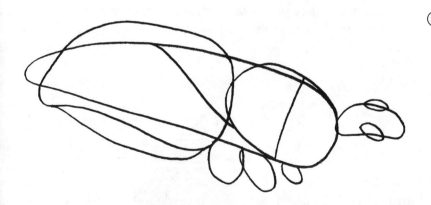

③ Add the large, slightly bulging eyes, the lower edge of the abdomen, a slanting line for the edge of the topmost wing, and three fat ovals for the three visible legs.

The assassin bug uses its stylet, a long, needle-like beak, to puncture its prey. After stabbing its prey, the bug injects its potent saliva into the prey's body, turning the prey's innards into fluid and allowing the assassin bug to suck them out.

MORE SCIENCE: Some species of assassin bugs suck blood, and attack humans and other mammals. Although assassin bugs inflict a very painful bite, the bite is not fatal to humans. However, some species do transmit an organism that causes New World Sleeping Sickness, a disease marked by tiredness, tremors, and extreme weight loss.

④ Add two curved lines directly behind the head and the longer portions of the legs. Also draw in the long pointed beak.

When its beak is not in use, it is neatly tucked into a narrow groove between the bug's front legs.

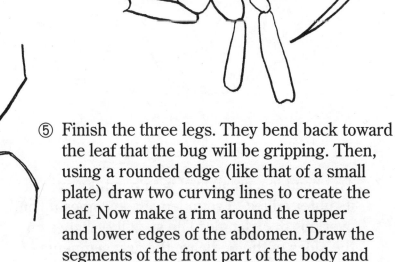

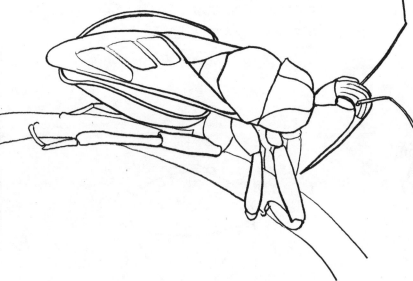

⑤ Finish the three legs. They bend back toward the leaf that the bug will be gripping. Then, using a rounded edge (like that of a small plate) draw two curving lines to create the leaf. Now make a rim around the upper and lower edges of the abdomen. Draw the segments of the front part of the body and the pattern on the wing. The head is grooved from the top to the beak, and the antennae have long sections like twigs. Erase all unneeded lines.

Half of the assassin bug's wings are transparent, and they cross over each other on top of the bug when it is at rest.

⑥ This is a red and black insect with a shiny, hard outer shell. You can make it look shiny by leaving white highlights on the highest parts of the back and the ridges of the wings, as well as by keeping white streaks on the legs. Draw in the details of the curving leaf.

The habitats of the assassin bug include grasslands, shrubs, meadows, as well as other natural environments such as deserts.

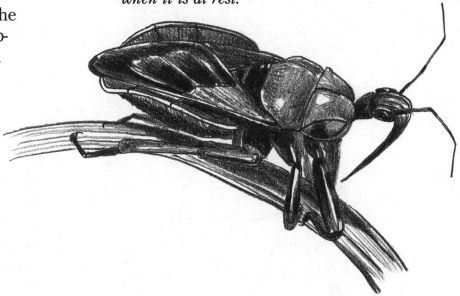

DRAWING TIP: Notice how this bug looks more lifelike if you draw the bug's shadow on the leaf.

The Harlequin Bug is a member of the stinkbug family—the skunks of the insect world. It is easily

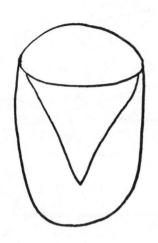

① The body (and wing area) of this bug form an oval that is flattened along the top edge. Make a curved line at the upper part of the oval to make a horizontal egg shape. Then connect a triangle to it.

The unpleasant scent given off by stinkbugs is not harmful to those who smell it. The odor is used simply to discourage potential predators who think that a stinkbug might make a tasty snack.

② The head is a small oval with beadlike eyes at its outer edges. A rounded shape comes up and overlaps the triangle. The sticklike shapes on the sides of the body are the first segments of the legs.

Harlequin bugs are only 0.35 to 0.45 inch (9 to 11.5 millimeters) in length. Their colors range from a dark blue to a glossy black with spots of orange and red.

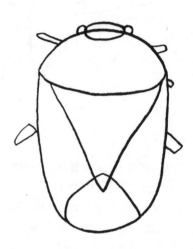

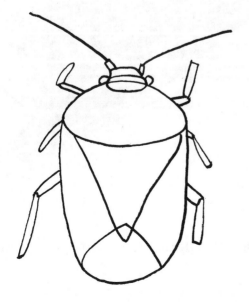

③ Add a top extension to the head oval. From it comes the rather stout antennae. Add the second, longer sections of the legs.

Lacking a pupal stage in its development, the harlequin bug develops through a process known as incomplete metamorphosis. Unlike a larva, which goes through complete metamorphosis, the young nymph in incomplete metamorphosis closely resembles the adult that it will become.

recognized by its shield shape and the foul odor it produces.

④ The feet end in two curving claws each. Draw in segments of the antennae.

The stinkbug family has over 5,000 species. Although most species are plant feeders, some prey on other insects as their food.

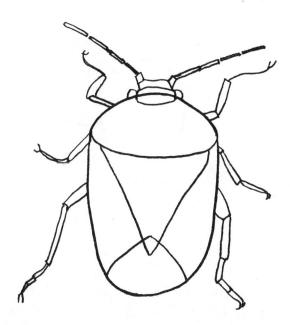

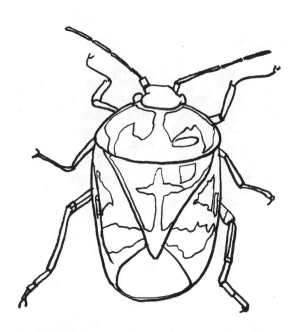

⑤ Erase extra lines and draw in the shapes of the black blotches on wing cases, the forepart of the body, and the legs.

Because they destroy crops of cabbage and other leafy vegetables, farmers consider harlequin bugs to be pests. Harlequin bugs are found most often across the southern part of the United States.

⑥ Darken the entire bug, including the legs, but leave white patches for the shiny highlights. There will be some on the eyes, the back of the head, the upper body, the center wing covering, and along the top edges of the legs. This bug is black and a rich tomato red.

Adult harlequin bugs go into a type of hibernation during the winter.

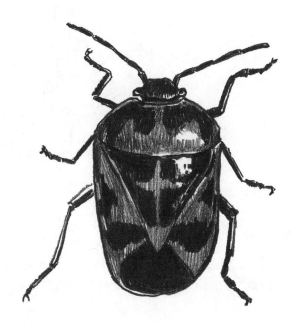

41

The Black Widow is one of the few poisonous spiders that are considered to be truly harmful to humans. It

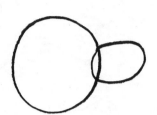

① The abdomen of this spider is almost a perfect circle, and its head area is a thick oval that overlaps one side of the abdomen.

Spiders are arachnids, and not considered insects. They have eight legs and two main body parts, while insects have six legs and three main body parts.

② Draw the four leg sections on the far side of the body. They all attach under the head area. Then add the two tiny leglike structures at the right.

The two small leglike shapes at the front of the black widow's body are called pedipalps. They help the spider handle its food.

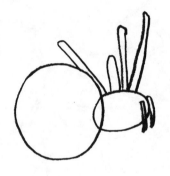

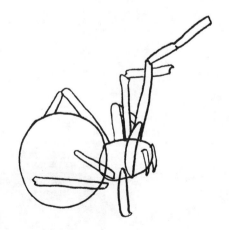

③ Add the four nearer leg segments and the second joints of the farther legs, overlapping as shown.

Only the female black widow is dangerous. If not treated by a doctor, the poison from her bite can sometimes kill a human. Half the size of the females, the male black widow is harmless.

MORE SCIENCE: Why is the black widow called a "widow?" The female has an eerie habit of killing and eating the male after mating, which leaves her a *widow*.

can be found in both tropical and moderate climates, including parts of the southern United States.

---

④ Continue to add the next segments to the nearer legs and the very slender down-curving tips of the three legs at the upper right.

While its bite may be fatal, the female black widow is not aggressive. It will usually try to run when it feels threatened, but when it gets cornered or is trying to protects its eggs, it will bite.

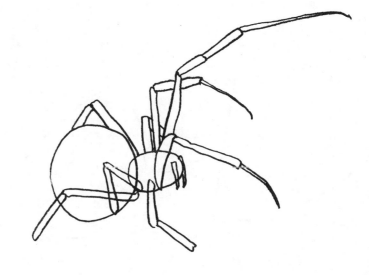

⑤ Add the slender tips of the three remaining legs to finish them, and erase the extra lines. Because there are so many narrow shapes overlapping, it might be easier to draw the final out-lines in dark non-smudging ink, and then go back and erase any unwanted pencil lines. That way you can erase over the whole drawing and not lose any of the final ink lines.

The mature black widow female is jet black and has a very distinct red mark in the shape of an hourglass on the underside of her abdomen. Her male counterpart has four pairs of red dots along both sides of his abdomen.

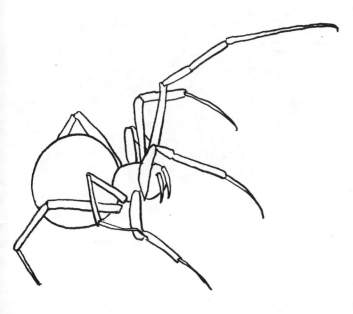

⑥ The black widow is a beautiful glossy black. Fill in the dark areas heavily. Leave a roundish white highlight on the abdomen, as well as streaks on the legs in order to show the spider's shine.

Once it has built its web, a black widow will rarely stray far from it. Its web may be found in fields, under logs and fallen leaves, or in undisturbed corners of garages and storage bins.

The Harvestman, commonly called a daddy longlegs, looks like its relative, the spider, but it has a rounder

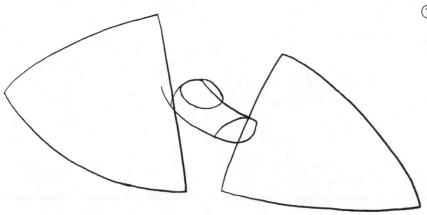

① Begin with a curved tube for the body. On either side of the body, place a triangular shape—these will be the guidelines for the long legs. Add an oval on the tube for the rear portion of the body.

When caught by a predator, a daddy longlegs sometimes attempts to escape by shedding one of its long legs. After the leg falls off, it continues to squirm, hopefully distracting the captor's attention long enough to give it time to escape.

② Draw three small rectangles where the legs attach, and a thicker rectangle at the left end of the tube for the stout rear leg. The small circle at the right and the curving oval are the first joints of the claw legs.

A daddy longlegs has tiny fluid-producing glands that secrete a foul-tasting fluid that makes it unappetizing to its predator, the spider. Once a spider tastes the fluid, it will run from the daddy longlegs and try to rid itself of the bad taste.

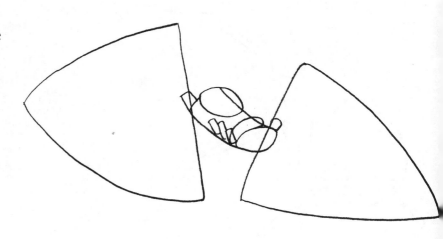

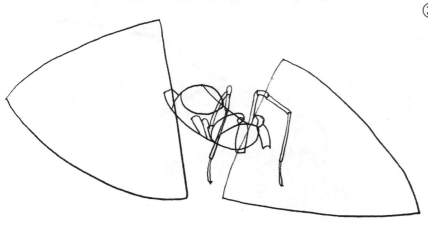

③ Because the legs are so long and easy to confuse, draw them one pair at a time. First draw the slender jointed front legs that end with a pair of tiny hooks. Notice the location of the bends and feet in relation to the triangular outlines. Add the thick second joint of the claw legs.

Daddy longlegs' favorite dwelling spots are wooded areas. While active at night, they usually hide under leaves, rocks, or in the underbrush of trees during the day.

44

body and longer, more slender legs than the spider. It is the harvestman's eight very long, thin legs that give it its nickname.

④ Add the last rounded joints of the claw legs. Then draw the second pair of long slender legs.

Daddy longlegs need plenty of water to survive. Direct sunlight quickly drains their bodies of moisture, causing these arachnids to dry out and become slow and tired. If they do not find water soon, they continue to dry up, and soon die.

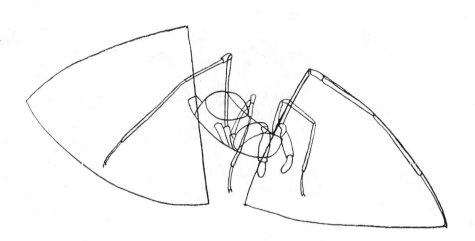

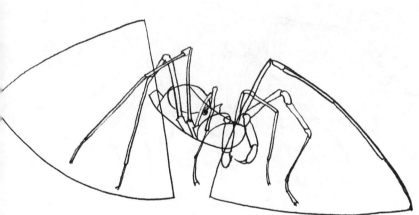

⑤ Finish the claw legs by adding the thorn-like claws. Add the arachnid's one visible eye, seen through the bend of its right front leg. Next to that is part of the other eye, only seen as a sharp ridge. Now add the third pair of legs. Notice the leg to the far right falls entirely along the triangular shape you drew on that side, and the leg on the left attaches to the last of the small rectangles against the body.

These arachnids feed on plants, dead insects, and may even eat other daddy longlegs. When in captivity, they will consume meat and bread.

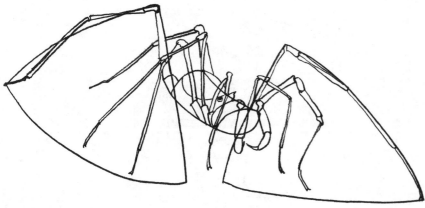

⑥ Draw in the rear legs, which are thicker near the body than the rest of the legs.

The harvestman should not be confused with one of its arachnid relatives, the daddy longlegs spider, that shares the same nickname. The difference between the two? The harvestman has an oval-shaped body and a segmented abdomen. The daddy longlegs spider, like all spiders, has a narrowing between its cephalothorax (fused head and thorax) and its unsegmented abdomen.

⑦ Erase all extra lines. (If you first go over the lines you want to keep in non-smearing dark ink, you can easily erase the extra pencil underneath.)

The second pair of legs, which are longer than the other three pairs, are especially important to daddy longlegs. They contain special sensory organs that warn of danger and tell where food may be located. Though the daddy longlegs could live if one leg of this second pair were detached, it would not survive very long if both were missing.

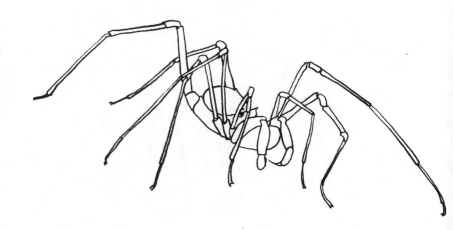

⑧ Make this arachnid look three-dimensional by adding darker shading on each leg section. Add the small foot segments and the sharp bumps on the back and claw legs. The harvestman has a rather pebbly shell, so you can suggest that with specks and pencil dots (a technique called stippling). Make the center of the eye dark. The dark areas in the front (just visible between the claw legs) are the folded fangs.

At the end of the summer, the female daddy longlegs places about thirty fertilized eggs into moist soil to prevent them from drying out. These eggs hatch in the springtime.

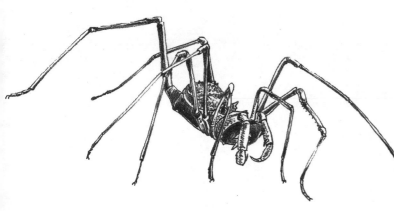

The Tarantula

has long been a target of fear. This hairy spider may look frightening and have a painful bite, but it has never been known to kill a human.

① This stocky spider is made up of lots of short chubby shapes all lined up together. Begin its abdomen with an oval and its cephalothorax (fused head and thorax) with a smaller, overlapping circle.

Some tarantula species will bite humans without being aggravated to do so. Male tarantulas are especially prone to bite during the mating season.

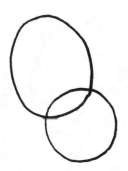

② Put in the first joints of each of the tarantula's eight legs. They all attach on the cephalothorax. Between the two sets of front legs on top of the cephalothorax, draw a round, stubby triangle. This is what you can see of the fangs from this top view.

Most often, it is a hungry tarantula that uses its bite. The spider grabs its prey with its jaws and injects venom through its fangs. Once the venom begins to affect its victim, the tarantula feeds.

③ Add the second row of leg joints, slightly overlapping the first joints. Draw the space between the two fangs.

Like all spiders, tarantulas are predators. They prey on insects, especially pests, including crickets and grasshoppers, such as the locust. They will also feed on small animals like mice, birds, or lizards.

④ Put in the two small eyes on top of the spider's head and a triangle area that will be darker than the rest of the head. Add the next section of leg joints. The two "tails" you see are part of the silk-making equipment of the tarantula.

Tarantulas differ slightly from other spiders. They have four lung slits instead of two. Also, while most spiders' jaws move side to side, those of the tarantula move up and down.

⑤ Go on to the next segments of the legs, and begin sketching the shorter palps, which are feelers on each side of the fangs.

To scare off predators, the tarantula rears up on its hind legs and rubs its front legs together, creating a hissing sound. If the predator still persists, the tarantula will take the spiky hairs, called satae (see-tee), off its abdomen and throw them at its hunter. These barbed hairs will stick in the face or paws of the attacker and cause a burning itch.

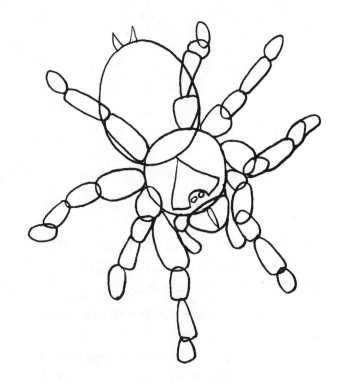

⑥ Finish the two front legs with oval feet, and the palps with a rounded log shape. Erase overlapping lines.

Although the tarantula has functioning silk glands, it does not use them to spin a web on which to live. Instead, it digs a hole, called a burrow, to serve as its home.

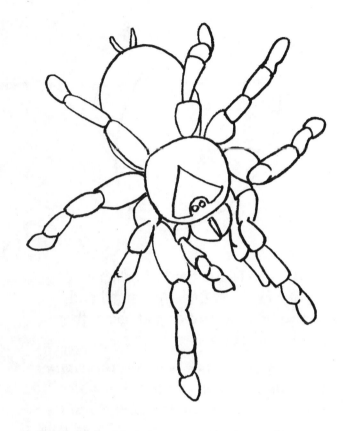

⑦ This large spider is covered with black and reddish hairs. Draw the hairs all over the body. The fur should curve slightly toward the leg it grows on, and the body fur should round in the same direction as the body curves.

A tarantula uses its silk glands to create a soft bed to lie on during its molting process. Tarantulas molt about four times a year during the first two years of life. After that they molt only about twice per year. Molting is a very vulnerable time for spiders, since they are unable to protect themselves from their enemies.

MORE SCIENCE: Most spiders live for about one year, but female tarantulas have the longest life span of all—they may survive up to thirty years!

Ticks

belong to the same Arachnida class as spiders, scorpions, and mites. Because they feed on other living organisms, ticks are parasites.

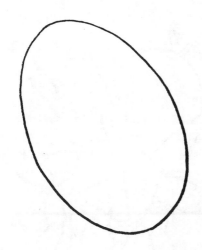

① Start with an egg shape.

There are two types of ticks—hard ticks and soft ticks. Hard ticks suck the blood of mammals, birds, reptiles, and amphibians. Soft ticks feed off the blood of poultry and other birds.

② Add the two triangular "wing" shapes, part of a circle at the egg's small end, and two floating circles just above this narrow end of the egg.

The life cycle of a tick is completed within about one year. It begins with a female swelling herself to capacity with a host's blood. She then seeks out a male, and they mate. After mating, the male dies and the female leaves the host.

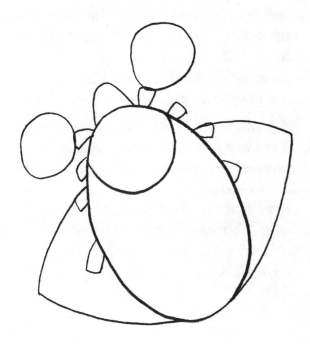

③ Connect the circles to the body with wedge shapes, then use more wedges to form the bases of the other legs. Add the blunt triangle for the head.

The female lays as many as 18,000 eggs in leaves or on the ground in a wooded area. Shortly afterward, the female adult tick also dies.

MORE SCIENCE: If a tick is unable to find a host, its life cycle will take longer to complete. Ticks will hibernate through the winter and can survive for months or even years without food.

Their only food is the blood of their host organisms.

---

④ Go on to the second and third segments of the legs, and draw the inside edges of the curved front legs. Draw the two flattened sides of the head.

Once an egg hatches, the six-legged larva will crawl up a bush or a grass stalk and wait for a host to pass by. When an acceptable host arrives, the larva grabs hold and clings to its fur, feathers, or skin. The larva then pierces the skin with its sharp beak, called a hypostome, and begins sucking blood.

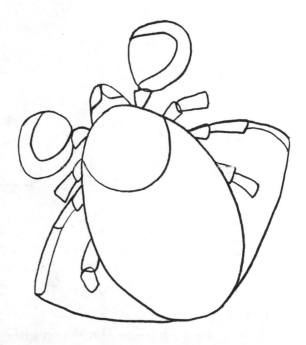

⑤ Put on the final hooklike feet. Draw slightly curving lines on the body to show where it is grooved. Also add the segments on the curved front legs. Erase any extra lines.

Once filled with blood, the larva falls to the ground to begin its first molt. When the molt is complete, a nymph with eight clawed legs emerges. It, too, finds a host, sucks blood, and falls to the ground. When the nymph molts, it turns into an adult tick.

⑥ Shade in the tick, whose upper back area is dark with a pitted surface. The legs are shiny and dark. The rest of the tick is pale and almost transparent. Shade the body gently so it looks light-colored.

The mouthpart of a tick consists of a rostrum, an anchoring organ covered with hooks, and sharp mandibles. Its abdomen is joined to the cephalothorax and is unsegmented.

Scorpions

often scare humans because of their appearance. This 4- to 5-inch-long (10 to 13 centimeters) arachnid has two large pincers that function like claws, as well as a fear-inspiring

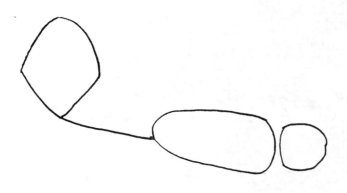

① Draw a bullet shape pointing left, and attach a slightly longer broken line. Construct a blunt diamond on the broken line. This will be the tail. For the head, draw a slightly squared circle, flattened on one end, near the other end of the bullet.

Of the forty species of scorpions in the United States, only a few inflict a sting that contains a venom that is deadly to people. Other countries have a greater number of dangerous species.

② Copy the two winglike shapes on either side of the head for the pincers. The scorpion's right pincer will appear much larger than the left. Then draw in the first segments of six of the eight rear legs.

Scorpions live only in dry and warm tropical climates. These arachnids become inactive in cold weather.

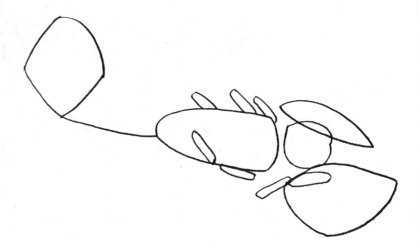

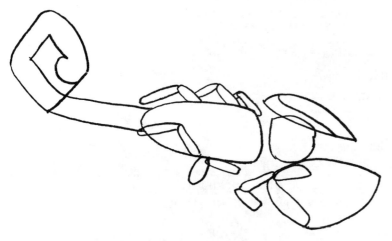

③ Draw in the upper edge of the tail section and add the second joint of each leg, including that of the front claws.

Like many other arachnids and insects, scorpions are active at night, when they hunt for spiders and insects to eat.

MORE SCIENCE: The female scorpion does not deposit her eggs. Instead, the eggs mature inside of her, and she gives birth to live scorpions. These weak, white scorpions climb aboard their mother's back and remain there for a few days. Then, following their first molt, they shed the special pad they had used for riding, and fall from their mother's back to begin their own trek in life.

stinger at the end of its abdomen. Curled upward and over its back, this stinger can cause a painful and sometimes deadly wound to humans.

④ Put in the last long bead shape of the legs and the claws. Draw the sections on the tail so it appears to curl up tightly on itself. Then draw the clawlike stinger at the end of the tail. Attach the claw legs to the head area, and draw the foremost small leg within the curve of the claw leg.

The scorpion uses its front pincers to catch its prey. If the victim battles for its life, it also will be stung by the scorpion before being eaten.

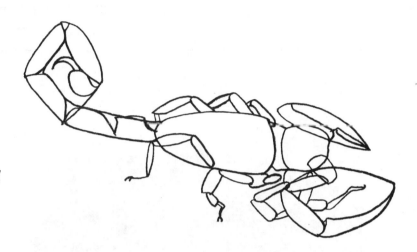

⑤ Finish the body by drawing lines for the body sections. Then add the small bump in the center of the head that holds the simple eyes. Erase any unneeded lines.

When preparing to mate, male scorpions seem to perform a "dance." When the male finds a fertile female, he closes his front pincers around her pincers and then, using his sensory organs, guides her to a suitable place to mate.

⑥ Make the legs and body of the scorpion look three-dimensional by grouping short hatching lines along their lower edges for shadows. Make lines darker and closer together where you think there would be darker shadows.

A male scorpion fertilizes a female by depositing his reproductive fluids (which are contained in a packet) onto a rock. He then pulls the female onto the packet on the rock. This allows his fluid sac to enter her body, dissolve, and fertilize her eggs.

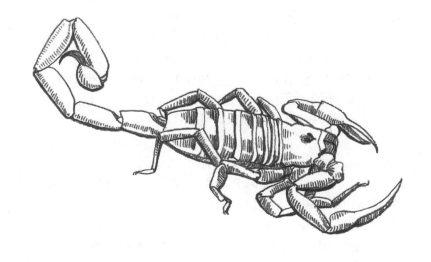

Backgrounds

Once you have completed a drawing, you may want to put your insect or arachnid in a setting. These creatures live in a variety of different settings, but you can add all sorts of things to make the scenery unusual and interesting. Nature magazines or books on insects and arachnids will show you environments in which these animals live. Or, use your imagination! Here are some suggestions for creating different settings.

MAGAZINE BACKGROUNDS

If you like to cut and paste, ask your family for some old magazines you can cut up. If your insect or arachnid lives around people, cut out a picture of a food or utensil so it looks like your drawing is in the same space as the photograph. You also can make a crazy collage by finding pictures of various sizes to add to the composition. Try to cut them out so as little of their original background shows as possible.

Glue sticks are a tidy way to apply adhesive. Place the cutout facedown on a piece of scrap paper. If you hold the cutout with one finger and stroke outward from the center with the glue stick you'll have the best chance of spreading the glue evenly and not tearing or ruffling up the paper's edges.

PAINTED BACKGROUNDS

You don't need a paintbrush to add these painted backgrounds! To create a ground texture use an old sponge, crumpled paper (like paper towels), or even the pattern on the fingertips of rubber gloves. Dip the material lightly in some paint you have spread in a jar lid, and print the pattern, overlapping until you have the darkness and texture you want. Practice on scrap paper until you have an idea of how it will look. If your drawing is large enough, you can use this painting method to make a texture on the insect or arachnid, itself. Be sure to leave space around the edges of your creature or it will disappear in the pattern!

TEXTURED BACKGROUNDS

If you want to create a textured background, first draw your animal on a thin piece of paper. Place a textured object (such as sandpaper) under the section of your paper where you want the texture to appear. Now grab a pencil with a soft lead. Then, using the side of the pencil lead, rub lightly and evenly over the area. To create a wood pattern use rough-surfaced wood (unpainted works best). You can use anything, from the side of a key to paperclips. Move the paper slightly so the textures of the objects overlap for interesting effects. Again, be sure to leave space around your insect or arachnid so that it doesn't disappear in your rubbed texture.

SHADOWED BACKGROUNDS

By adding shadows in the right places, your insects will leap off the page! Imagine where the shadow of your insect or arachnid would fall underneath the body, legs, and wings. Then fill in those areas with a dark pencil. You can copy pictures of plants or rocky areas for realistic backgrounds—keeping the insect the lightest part of the drawing—or you can make up a setting. Work carefully, making sure you fill in every area you want dark. Also shade up to the edge of the insect. Remember to draw the shadows touching the insect's feet where they meet the surface.

Bringing Your Animal to Life

Here are more tips on how to put life into your drawings. Keep in mind that the most realistic drawings combine several finishing techniques. You can practice and experiment with your own favorite combinations!

CONTOUR DRAWING

Even if you don't plan to fill in your drawing with color or texture, you can make your animal look more solid by changing the darkness and width of its outlines. For example, note the difference in the line weight within the drawing of the cicada nymph. The lower edges of the body and legs are thicker to suggest shadows. The faint lines wrapping around the abdomen grow increasingly darker as they get closer to the underside. Also, whenever a line bends or meets another line it thickens. This technique not only makes the insect shape appear more three-dimensional, but it also makes the drawing more fun to look at.

CAST SHADOWS

The simplest thing you can do to make your drawing look rounded and real is to give it a shadow. To do this, you must imagine where the shadow of its form would be if the insect were resting on a flat surface with light coming from above. The hercules beetle casts a shadow that extends from between its feet to under its helmet. Notice that the underside of the body is all in shadow, and the cast shadow gets darker in the areas where the body is closest to the ground. Otherwise it is fairly even. Remember, the shadows touch any part of the insect that contacts the ground.

LIGHT FIGURE, DARK BACKGROUND

You'll be surprised by how rounded your insect looks if you simply darken the space behind it. By darkening the space behind this silkworm moth, you can create a rounded, three-dimensional effect. You can imagine looking out a window and seeing this moth flying in the night sky. Adding shading on the moth itself adds to the rounded look, as well as the effect of being in the space rather than on top of a flat black shape.

Making Your Animal Seem Larger (or Smaller)

How do you make an animal in a small drawing seem larger? Or an animal in a huge picture seem smaller? The following techniques will show you how.

THE HORIZON LINE

To show how big your creature is in a drawing, add a ground line or horizon line across your picture. If your insect or arachnid is very small, you can make it appear larger by drawing it inside a matchbox. This would place the horizon line where the side of the box meets the floor. Normally the horizon line is on the viewer's eye level. So, if the top of the insect or arachnid's body is drawn higher than the horizon line, it seems larger. If the horizon is near the top of your picture and the insect or arachnid is toward the bottom, it seems smaller.

horizon line

ADDING OBJECTS FOR SCALE

FANTASY SCALE

Another way to indicate your insect or arachnid's size is to include objects whose size most people know. For example, people know that biplanes and falcons are much larger than all types of insects. Drawing the dragonfly flying with these two objects makes the dragonfly appear much larger than it is in reality.

REALISTIC SCALE

If a person has never seen a praying mantis, it is hard for him or her to know exactly how big one is. So, if you draw the insect as it might actually be, on a plant whose size most people know, you can convey an accurate measurement of this creature. Don't forget the shadows so the insect really seems to be resting on the petals.

Tips on Color

Your picture will stand out from the rest of the crowd if you use these helpful tips on how to add color to your masterpiece!

TRY WHITE ON BLACK

For a different look, try working on black construction paper or art paper. Then, instead of pencil, use white chalk, white prismacolor pencil, or poster paint. With this technique, you'll need to concentrate on drawing the light areas in your picture rather than the dark ones. Because the silverfish is a pale-colored insect with a silvery color, this coloring method is perfect for it.

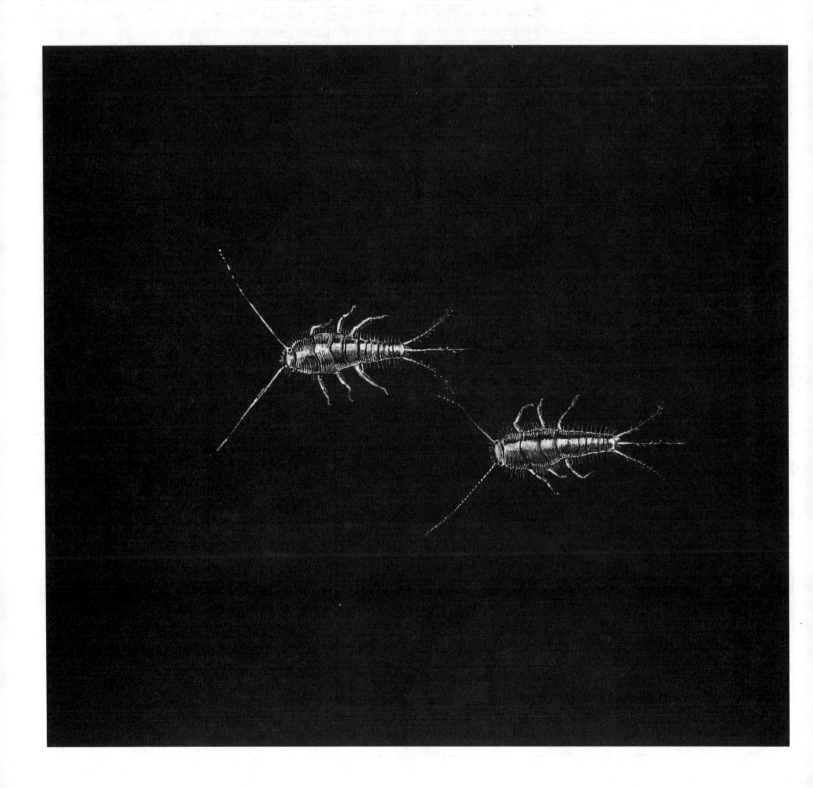

TRY BLACK AND WHITE ON GRAY (OR TAN)

You don't need special gray or tan paper from the art store for this technique. Instead, try cutting apart the inside of a grocery bag or a cereal box. This time, your background is a middle tone (neither light nor dark). Sketch your insect in black, then use white to make highlights. Add black for the shadows. Don't completely cover up the tan or gray of the cardboard. Let it be the middle tone within your illustration. With this technique, your pictures can have a very finished look with a minimal amount of drawing!

TRY COLOR

Instead of using every color in your marker set or your colored pencil set, try drawing in black for shadows, white for highlights, and one color for a middle tone. This third color blended with the white creates a fourth color. You will be surprised how professional your drawing will look.

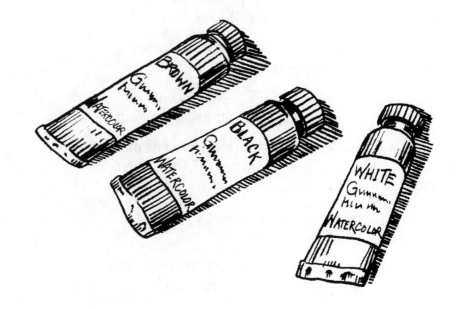

Glossary

Africanized honeybees: the name given to the offspring of African queen bees that mated with European species of honeybees

arachnid: a creature that has eight legs, no antennae, and a two-part body made up of a cephalothorax and an abdomen

auditory: related to hearing

burrow: hole in the ground used for shelter, such as that built by the tarantula

caste: a level of specialization in a colony of social insects, such as reproductives and workers

caterpillar: the larva of a moth or butterfly

cephalothorax: the body region of arachnids made up of a fused head and thorax

cocoon: the silken case where a pupa forms during complete metamorphosis

colonies: settlements of the same species of insects living and working together as a group

complete metamorphosis: development of insects in four distinct stages: egg, larva, pupa, and adult

compound eye: the major insect eye that is made up of many tiny lenses

crop: the first chamber in the ant stomach that acts as the food-storing "social stomach"

donor ant: the ant that shares its full crop with other hungry ants

drone: the male bee that fertilizes the eggs of the female bee

family: a biological grouping of insects smaller than an order, but bigger than a genus

fore: at the front

host: an animal or plant on which parasites feed

incomplete metamorphosis: development of insects in three separate stages: egg, nymph (larva), and adult

larval stage: the second stage in the development of insects. The larva is the immature insect; larvae is plural.

maggot: the larva of flies

mandible: lower jaw

metamorphosis: the changes an insect undergoes in its development from egg to adult

midgut: the middle section of the ant's digestive tract

molt: to shed the outer covering, or exoskeleton

mound: a raised hill of earth, sand, or rocks used as a home for ants

nits: lice eggs

nymph: the immature, wingless stage of insects who undergo incomplete metamorphosis; often look like miniature versions of the adult

ocelli: simple insect eyes that contain a single lense

öotheca: a firm-walled egg case, such as from a cockroach

opaque: not able to be seen through

order: a biological grouping of insects, larger than a family

parasite: a plant or animal that lives off another living creature (such as fleas, lice, and ticks)

pest: a plant or animal that is considered destructive

pheromone: a substance released by animals and insects such as ants, so they may recognize members of their own species

predator: a hunter; a creature that hunts other creatures for food

prey: the victim of a hunter

pupa: the third stage in complete metamorphosis, during which an insect undergoes many physical changes, usually within a cocoonlike structure

queen bees: the fertile females in the reproductive caste that reign over a hive

species: a category of biological classification; members of a species have common characteristics that group them together under a common name

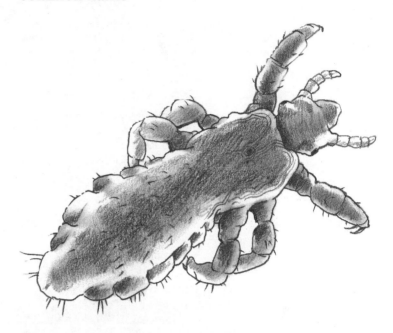

stridulating: the rubbing together of two body parts, such as legs against wings, to produce a specific sound (often used as a mating call)

stylet: a long, needlelike beak used to puncture the skin of a host

swarm: 1) a large group of insects; 2) a group of flying insects, such as bees, that are searching for a new nest site

transparent: able to be seen through

thorax: segmented, middle body section bearing the legs and wings

true locusts: the migratory grasshopper, which is considered a pest

venom: poisonous matter secreted by some insects and arachnids

worker bees: the caste of sterile females who perform the majority of work in a bee colony

wrigglers: mosquito larvae, given this name because of their squirmy feeding and escape behavior